THE BROWN BAG LUNCH

A Collection of
Recipes and Tips
for the Perfect
Portable Lunch

Susan Epstein

Macmillan • USA

MACMILLAN
A Simon & Schuster Macmillan Company
1633 Broadway
New York, NY 10019-6785

Library of Congress Cataloging-in-Publication Data is available upon request.

ISBN 0-02-861294-9

Design by Rachael McBrearty

Illustrations by Deborah Haley Melmon

Manufactured in the United States of America
10 9 8 7 6 5 4 3 2 1

With special thanks and love to:

My husband, Harvey, for his confidence in me and his willingness to try just about anything for lunch

My children, Stephanie and Gregory, for making cooking and baking "our special time"

My mother, Esty Moskowitz, for always believing in me

My dear friends and family, who tested more sandwiches, salads, and brownies than they can count

And, last but not least, the crushed, soggy tuna sandwich, for indigestion and inspiration

INTRODUCTION

LET'S BROWN BAG IT!

Today, people live on the run, grabbing lunch whenever they can. Eating a leisurely lunch tends to take a backseat to other areas of our hectic lives. Time has become more and more precious.

And lunch has become more and more expensive. A high-fat, fast-food lunch costs about five dollars and a gourmet salad or sandwich can cost even more. Grabbing lunch puts a big dent in your budget.

Bringing lunch from home can save time and money, but what about taste? Are we destined to eat soggy tuna sandwiches in exchange for more time and money?

This book is the perfect answer: a collection of recipes and tips, which proves bringing lunch can taste wonderful and give us greater control over our diets. So, throw away that soggy tuna sandwich. Try these terrific recipes and you'll be sure to grab your little brown bag on your way out every morning. And so will your spouse or kids. Just keep in mind, once friends see what you are having for lunch, they may want to share!

Tips for the Perfect Brown-Bag Lunch

Okay, you want to create the perfect portable lunch. Now it is time to plan your menu, purchase ingredients, prepare your culinary masterpieces, pack them, and finally eat. Whether you are a novice or an everyday brown bagger, this book will be your guide to the perfect brown-bag lunch—fast, delicious, and affordable.

The Brown Bagger's Pantry, Freezer, and Refrigerator of Staples

There is always something delicious to make when you have a variety of nonperishables, frozen cooked foods, and basic refrigerator items at your fingertips. A well-stocked pantry saves preparation time and cuts down on the number of supermarket trips you need to make.

The Brown Bagger's Well-Stocked Pantry

- olive oil
- sesame oil
- flavored oils
- vegetable cooking spray
- sun-dried tomatoes
- roasted peppers
- marinated artichokes
- canned fish
- flavored vinegars
- Dijon mustard
- soy sauce
- pimento
- canned soup
- mayonnaise
- honey
- dried fruits
- variety of nuts
- tahini
- dried herbs and spices
- freshly ground black pepper
- peanut butter
- jams and preserves
- variety of sugars
- variety of flours
- vanilla extract
- variety of chocolate chips
- crisp Chinese noodles
- variety of pastas
- variety of rices
- variety of condiments
- variety of crackers, rice cakes, flat breads
- variety of pretzels, chips
- variety of fat-free and regular salad dressings
- juice boxes

The Brown Bagger's Freezer

Freeze cooked foods in individual portions. This saves lots of time on a daily basis.

- Poached Chicken Breasts (page 2)
- Grilled Chicken (page 5)
- Pesto Dressings (page 16)
- homemade breads, sliced
- store-bought breads, sliced
- homemade brownies
- homemade cookies
- salad dressings without mayonnaise
- soups
- butter
- leftovers
- cheeses
- refreezable ice blocks
- juice boxes

The Brown Bagger's Refrigerator of Staples

Other items will be needed depending on your weekly menu.

- fresh herbs
- fresh vegetables
- fresh fruit
- cream cheese
- Grilled Vegetables (page 3)

- assorted cold cuts
- assorted cheeses
- juice boxes and assorted drinks
- horseradish
- eggs

Timesaving and Moneysaving Tips

Let's face it: When it comes to time and money, most of us could use a little more. Here are a few tips to help you save some of your precious time and dollars during preparation.

Saving Time

- Freeze breads, cooked chicken, leftovers, Pesto Dressings (page 16), baked treats, and soups in individual or weekly portions. Use as needed for up to one month.
- Grill poultry or vegetables on a weekly basis and store in separate tightly covered plastic containers. Refrigerate for up to 1 week.
- Make a weekly shopping list and purchase everything you will need. If you don't have an ingredient or run out, improvise. Frequent trips to the supermarket waste time.
- Have a well-stocked Brown Bagger's Pantry (above).
- Have plenty of ready-made salad dressings on hand in case you run out of homemade or you are pressed for time.
- Plan your lunches on a weekly basis. This avoids the early morning lunch panic that wastes time and usually results in a peanut butter sandwich.

Saving Money

- Purchase nonperishable sale items in large quantity.
- Purchase perishable items like fruits and vegetables about every five days to avoid spoilage.

- Frequent the large food warehouses that are popping up all over the country. Comparison-shop with your local supermarket; prices vary according to specials offered.
- Avoid impulse purchases, which can put a big dent in the monthly budget.
- Do not use charge cards to pay for food unless you pay the bill in full on a monthly basis. Finance charges add up.
- Buy fruits and vegetables that are in season; they have superior quality and are cheaper.
- Stay away from individually packaged foods; buy larger packages and divide into individual portions.
- Don't throw out small quantities of leftover food. See Leftovers (page 85) for ideas.
- Clip coupons for items you buy regularly.
- Try items packaged under the store brand or private label. If you are happy with the quality, these brands are usually much cheaper.
- Do not go shopping when you are hungry; anything looks good when your stomach is empty.
- Store food properly; you are wasting food and money if you buy large quantities of sale items and let them spoil.

Packing Tips

Once you have prepared the food, the next step is packing—correctly. At lunchtime, this will ensure that your meal will look and taste the same as when you packed it. Follow these tips and your brown-bag lunch will be perfect every time.

Equipment

- brown bags, lunch box, insulated bag
- a variety of plastic and microwavable containers with tight-fitting lids
- aluminum foil
- a variety of thermos bottles and jars
- self-sealing plastic bags
- plastic blocks of refreezable gel or ice substitute—"ice" blocks will keep food cold for several hours

Pack It Up

- Pack sandwiches in tightly sealed aluminum foil, self-sealing plastic baggies, or plastic sandwich containers. Reusing the containers will save you money in the long run and they are better for the environment.
- Pack salads and dressings in separate tightly sealed plastic containers. This will help the salad retain its fresh taste.
- Pack chips, cookies, brownies, breads, and other crushable foods in plastic containers or self-sealing plastic bags. Be sure to pack fragile foods at the top of the lunch bag to avoid crushing.

Keep It Cold

- Chill food for at least 1 hour before packing.
- Chill the lunch box or insulated bag before you pack it.
- Place frozen blocks of ice substitute on top of the food you want kept cold, or:
- Place frozen juice boxes on top of food you want kept cold. By lunchtime the juice will be thawed but cold, and it will have doubled as an ice pack. Be sure to wrap the boxes in paper before packing, because the boxes will get a little wet as they thaw.

- Beverages and cold soups should be packed in thermos bottles that have been refrigerated for at least 1 hour. Salad can also be packed in a chilled wide-mouth thermos.
- If possible, refrigerate the lunch when you get to your destination.

Keep It Hot

- Pack hot soups, stews, and leftovers in a preheated wide-mouth thermos. To preheat a thermos, fill it with boiling water, cover, and set aside while you prepare and heat the food. When the food is ready, pour out the hot water and then quickly pour in the hot food. Close tightly.
- If you have a microwave at your destination, pack foods in micro-wavable containers and heat them up at lunchtime for a satisfying hot lunch.

Menu Tips

When preparing your own lunch menus keep in mind the following:
- How much time do I have to prepare lunch this week?
- What is my lunch budget?
- How much money am I saving?
- Are there any special requests?
- Have I planned a balanced menu that meets my health goals?
- Am I offering a variety of foods?

Chapter One

THE BASICS

Included here is everything you need to get started—basic techniques, basic foods, basic fillings, breads, condiments, and basic spreads.

Remember, many of these foods can be frozen for up to a month or refrigerated for about a week. Simply plan your menu and set aside one hour on a weekly basis to prepare the basic foods you will need for the recipes throughout the book. (If you are making quick breads, you may need a little more time for baking.) Daily preparation will be minimal and you will have the satisfaction of always having something delicious for lunch.

POACHED CHICKEN BREASTS

1 to 2 pounds boneless, skinless chicken breasts, rinsed, cleaned, and patted dry

1¹/₂ tablespoons freshly squeezed lemon juice

salt, to taste

3 cups low-sodium chicken broth *or* ¹/₂ cup white wine mixed with 2¹/₂ cups water

1 tablespoon whole black peppercorns

1. Preheat the oven to 350°F.

2. Place the chicken in a single layer in a 9×13-inch baking pan. Drizzle the lemon juice over the chicken breasts. Season with salt.

3. Combine the chicken broth and peppercorns in a small pan; bring liquid to a boil. Remove from heat; pour over chicken.

Serving Suggestion

For a fast, delicious lunch, add poached chicken breasts to packaged salad and your favorite bottled dressing.

4. Bake, covered, until juices run clear when thickest part of chicken is cut, 30 minutes. Remove the chicken from the pan; discard the liquid, cool the chicken, and proceed with your favorite recipe.

Makes 1 to 2 pounds

Tip

Timesaving

Make a large batch of poached chicken and freeze the extra. As long as you have some on hand, you can have a gourmet lunch in minutes.

GRILLED VEGETABLES

Grilled vegetables are versatile, inexpensive, and excellent in a variety of sandwiches and salads. Simply vary your cooking time according to the thickness of vegetables.

I small eggplant, zucchini, or onion, cut crosswise into 1/2-inch-thick slices

salt

1/4 cup olive oil

I garlic clove, minced

I tablespoon freshly squeezed lemon juice

I teaspoon dried oregano

freshly ground black pepper, to taste

1. Place the eggplant slices on a baking sheet and lightly sprinkle salt* over each slice. Let stand at least 1 hour. Pat dry with paper towels.

2. Whisk together the oil, garlic, lemon juice, and oregano. Season with pepper and additional salt. Place the eggplant slices on the rack of the grill and brush lightly with the oil mixture.

3. Grill, turning once, basting occasionally with the oil mixture, for about 10 minutes. Cool. Refrigerate in an airtight container up to 1 week.

Makes about 2 cups

Tips

For grilling vegetables:
- Use a rack specifically made for grilling vegetables. This prevents vegetables from slipping through the grill grates.
- Watch closely to avoid burning.
- For low-calorie grilling, spray the vegetables with nonstick cooking spray and season with herbs.

* For grilled zucchini or onions, it is not necessary to salt prior to grilling.

ROASTED PEPPERS

4 red, yellow, orange, green, or any other variety of bell peppers

1. Preheat the broiler.

2. Wash and dry the peppers.

3. Broil the peppers, turning often, until skin is blackened and blistered, about 10 minutes.

4. Place peppers in a clean paper bag, close tightly, and let stand for 15 minutes.

5. Remove the peppers from the bag. Peel the skin off the peppers. Store in a container with a tight-fitting lid. Use within 1 week.

Tip

Timesaving

If you are pressed for time, store-bought roasted peppers can be substituted in any recipe with good results but a slightly different taste.

Tips

To quickly core and seed a pepper:
1. Cut it in half through the core.
2. Pull the core and seeds out in one piece.
3. Hit the back of the pepper with your hand to loosen any remaining seeds.

GRILLED CHICKEN

1/4 cup olive oil

1 garlic clove, minced

1 tablespoon freshly squeezed lemon juice

salt and freshly ground black pepper, to taste

1 pound boneless, skinless chicken breasts, rinsed, cleaned, and
   patted dry

nonstick cooking spray

1. Combine the oil, garlic, lemon juice, salt, and pepper in a small, nonreactive bowl. Add the chicken breasts; cover and refrigerate at least 2 hours.

2. Thirty minutes before serving, spray the grill rack with nonstick cooking spray. Preheat the grill. Place the chicken on the prepared grill rack. Grill, turning once, basting often with marinade, until juices run clear and no longer pink when center of the thickest piece of chicken is cut, about 8 minutes.

Variation

Substitute for marinade: Your favorite purchased or homemade marinade.

Makes about 1 pound

Tip

If you don't have a grill, broil the chicken, about 4 minutes per side. Make sure you baste it frequently so it does not dry out.

Cooking Tips

Before you begin:

• Make sure the grill rack is sprayed or oiled to prevent food from sticking.

• Make sure the food is all the same temperature to ensure even cooking.

RATATOUILLE

2 tablespoons olive oil

2 garlic cloves, minced

1/2 cup chopped onion

1 teaspoon Italian seasoning

1 eggplant, cut into 1/2-inch cubes

1/2 red bell pepper, cut into 1/2-inch squares

1 small zucchini, cut into 1-inch strips

1/2 pound chopped, seeded plum tomatoes (about 4 medium)

salt and freshly ground black pepper, to taste

Tip

Ratatouille keeps in the refrigerator for up to 1 week. It stands well on its own, with a tossed salad, or "dressed up" with other ingredients.

1. Combine the oil, garlic, onion, and Italian seasoning in a 3-quart microwavable casserole. Cover and microwave at High for 5 minutes.

2. Add the remaining ingredients and microwave at High for 8 minutes. Stir and cook for an additional 7 minutes. Stir and let stand for at least 5 minutes. Adjust seasoning.

Makes 2 to 4 servings

Cooking Tip

The ratatouille can also be prepared on the stove top. Heat the oil over medium heat. Sauté the ingredients from step 1 for 10 minutes. Add remaining ingredients and simmer for about 20 minutes or until soft.

Serving Suggestions

- Spread on thick black bread and sprinkle with goat cheese or fresh mozzarella. Top with arugula.
- Toss with chicken and cold pasta.
- Use in place of roasted peppers on your favorite sandwich.
- Use as a substitute topping for Stuffed Potatoes with Tuna and Cheddar Cheese (page 63).
- Use as an alternate filling for Cheddar and Tomato Quiche (page 60).

TUNA SALAD

Tuna, chicken, and egg salads are deliciously basic and simple. Put your personal stamp on each with a variety of garnishes and breads.

1/4 cup red or Vidalia onion, finely chopped

1/4 cup celery, coarsely chopped

1 can (7 1/2 ounces) tuna, drained and finely chopped

1/4 cup mayonnaise, Herb Mayonnaise (page 23), Horseradish Mayonnaise (page 22), or Dill Mayonnaise (page 23)

salt and freshly ground black pepper, to taste

1. Combine the onion, celery, and tuna in a large bowl.

2. Add the mayonnaise; season with salt and pepper. Mix well to coat thoroughly.

Makes 2 servings

Serving Suggestion

This salad is wonderful on black bread.

Variations

- Add sliced grapes.
- Add chopped hard-boiled eggs.
- Top with cheese slices.
- Substitute fat-free cottage cheese mixed with 1 tablespoon of Herb Mayonnaise (page 23) prepared with fat-free mayonnaise for a low-calorie salad.
- Top with tomato slices.

EGG SALAD

This version is inexpensive, easy to make, and a real treat for the taste buds. So indulge. It's terrific on black bread or an onion roll.

4 hard-boiled eggs, coarsely chopped
1/4 cup red onion, finely chopped
2 tablespoons Dijon Mayonnaise (page 22), or to taste
salt and freshly ground black pepper, to taste

1. Combine the eggs and onion in a bowl.

2. Add Dijon Mayonnaise to coat egg mixture, as desired. Season with salt and pepper.

Makes 2 to 3 servings

CHICKEN SALAD

1 1/2 cups cooked chicken, cubed or chopped
1/2 cup celery
1/4 cup mayonnaise
1 tablespoon freshly squeezed lemon juice
1 tablespoon fresh chopped dill, tarragon, chives, or parsley

1. Combine chicken and celery in a large bowl.

2. Mix the mayonnaise, lemon juice, and fresh herbs in a separate small bowl.

3. Combine the mayonnaise mixture with the chicken mixture; mix well.

Makes 2 servings

Variations

- Mix with sautéed chopped onions, sliced mushrooms, and a little flavored oil—hold the mayo.
- Mix with bacon slices, bacon bits, minced ham, or sliced prosciutto.
- Top with steamed green beans.
- Mix with 1 cup finely chopped spinach.
- Surround with blanched vegetables and cubed melon—a perfect diet meal when prepared with fat-free mayonnaise.

BANANA BREAD

1 1/4 cups whole wheat flour

1 teaspoon salt

1 teaspoon baking soda

1/2 cup unsalted butter, at room temperature

2/3 cup sugar

3 small ripe bananas, mashed (about 1 cup)

2 eggs, beaten

1/2 cup chopped nuts, mini-chocolate chips, or raisins (optional)

1. Preheat the oven to 350°F. Lightly grease an 8- or 9-inch loaf pan.

2. Combine the flour, salt, and baking soda in a small bowl. Set aside.

Tip

Quick breads are easy to make and can be frozen for up to 1 month. Wrap each slice in one layer of freezer wrap and one layer of aluminum foil or place the entire sliced loaf in a plastic freezer container.

3. Cream the butter and sugar in a large bowl until light. Add the mashed banana and eggs; mix well.

4. Add the flour mixture until just combined.

5. Add the nuts. Mix until just combined. Pour into prepared loaf pan.

6. Bake until a tester inserted in the center of the bread comes out clean, about 1 hour. Cool completely on a wire rack.

Makes 12 to 14 slices

Serving Suggestions

- cream cheese or peanut butter and strawberry jam
- Egg Salad (page 8) and thin slices of tomato
- peanut butter and apple slices
- a container of yogurt and a small fruit salad
- peanut butter and orange marmalade
- peanut butter and ham

PUMPKIN BREAD

1 1/2 cups all-purpose flour

1 teaspoon baking powder

1 teaspoon baking soda

1 teaspoon cinnamon

1/8 teaspoon nutmeg

1/2 teaspoon ground ginger

1/2 teaspoon salt

1 cup sugar

3/4 cup oil

2 eggs

1 cup (8 ounces) cooked and mashed or canned pumpkin

1/2 cup chopped walnuts (optional)

1. Preheat the oven to 350°F. Grease and flour a 9-inch loaf pan.

2. Sift together the flour, baking powder, baking soda, cinnamon, nutmeg, ginger, and salt. Set aside.

3. Beat the sugar and oil together in a large bowl. Add the eggs, one at a time, beating well after each addition.

4. Add the flour mixture to the egg mixture, 1/4 cup at a time, mixing well after each addition. Stir in the pumpkin and nuts, if desired.

5. Pour batter into prepared pan. Bake until a tester inserted in the center of the loaf comes out clean, 50 to 60 minutes. Invert and cool completely on a wire rack.

Makes 12 to 14 slices

Serving Suggestions

- turkey and Swiss cheese
- roast beef and chutney
- Flavored Cream Cheese (pages 14–15)
- smoked ham and Roasted Peppers (page 4)

WHOLE WHEAT
CARROT-WALNUT BREAD

This is a good bread for the kids—it's low in fat, sweet, and contains whole grains and vegetables. Add a healthy filling and you'll have a lunch that contains something from all the food groups.

1 1/2 cups whole wheat flour
1 teaspoon baking powder
1/4 teaspoon baking soda
1/4 teaspoon salt
1 teaspoon cinnamon
1 cup sugar
1/4 cup vegetable oil
1/2 cup applesauce
2 eggs
1 teaspoon vanilla
1 cup cooked carrots, puréed, or two (4 ounce) jars carrot baby food
1/2 cup chopped walnuts

1. Preheat the oven to 350°F. Grease and flour a 9-inch loaf pan.

2. Sift together the flour, baking powder, baking soda, salt, and cinnamon. Set aside.

3. Beat the sugar, oil, and applesauce together in a large bowl. Add the eggs, one at a time, beating well after each addition. Add the vanilla.

4. Add the flour mixture to the egg mixture, 1/4 cup at a time, mixing well after each addition. Stir in the carrots and nuts.

5. Pour batter into prepared pan. Bake until a tester inserted in the center of the loaf comes out clean, 50 to 60 minutes. Invert and cool completely on a wire rack.

Makes 12 to 14 slices

Serving Suggestions

- cottage cheese and Dried Fruit Compote (page 102)
- spread on Flavored Cream Cheese (pages 14–15)
- Waldorf Salad (page 48)
- Egg Salad (page 8)

CORN BREAD

1 cup yellow corn meal
1 cup all-purpose flour
$1/4$ cup sugar
$2^1/2$ teaspoons baking powder
$1/2$ teaspoon salt
2 eggs, lightly beaten
$1/2$ cup unsalted butter, melted
1 cup buttermilk

1. Preheat the oven to 400° F. Grease and flour 9-inch loaf pan.

2. Combine the corn meal, flour, sugar, baking powder, and salt in a large bowl.

3. Add the eggs and mix well. Stir in the butter and buttermilk. Mix until just combined.

4. Pour batter into prepared pan. Bake until tester inserted into the center comes out clean, 40 minutes. Invert and cool completely on a wire rack.

Serving Suggestions

A slice of this bread is a wonderful accompaniment to spicy salads, soups, chili, or stew. It also makes good stuffing.

Makes 16 servings

Variations

Add:
- $1/2$ cup chopped bacon
- 1 cup cooked corn kernels
- $3/4$ cup grated cheddar cheese
- $1/4$ cup canned or fresh chopped green chilies
- $1/4$ cup finely chopped red pepper
- $1/2$ cup chopped sun-dried tomatoes, packed in oil, drained

FRUITY MUFFINS

2 cups all-purpose flour
2 teaspoons baking powder
1/2 teaspoon salt
1/2 cup sugar
2 eggs, lightly beaten
1/2 cup melted butter
1 cup milk
1 cup mixed fresh or frozen berries
1 teaspoon grated lemon zest*

Serving Suggestion

These muffins are delicious on their own, packed with a salad, or cut in half, filled, and made into a "muffinwich," as in Cheddar Cheese and Smoked Turkey Muffinwich (page 83).

1. Preheat the oven to 400° F.

2. Whisk together the flour, baking powder, and salt in a large bowl.

3. In a small bowl whisk together the sugar, eggs, butter, and milk. Add to the dry mixture and mix until just combined.

4. Add the fruit and lemon zest. Fill greased muffin tins 2/3 full.

5. Bake at 400° F. for 20 to 25 minutes or until a tester inserted in the center comes out clean.

Makes about 18 muffins

Variations

For fruit muffins, use 1 cup of chopped fruit and 1 teaspoon of flavoring. Try:
- strawberries and grated orange zest
- chopped apples, raisins, and cinnamon

For savory muffins, use only 1 to 2 tablespoons of sugar, 1 teaspoon of dried herbs, and 1/2 cup of cheese. Try:
- chopped apples and cheddar cheese
- chopped tomatoes, Parmesan cheese, and basil

---

* The zest of the lemon is the outermost peel without any of the pith (white membrane). To remove zest, use a zester or the fine side of a vegetable grater.

FLAVORED CREAM CHEESE

Raisin Cream Cheese

8 ounces cream cheese, softened
1/4 cup raisins
1/2 teaspoon cinnamon
1/4 cup finely chopped walnuts (optional)
1/4 cup chopped dates (optional)

Combine all ingredients in a small bowl; mix well. Store in a container with a tight-fitting lid. Store in the refrigerator up to 2 weeks.

Chunky Fruit Cream Cheese

4 ounces cream cheese, softened
3/4 cup chopped strawberries or blueberries
1 teaspoon sugar, or to taste
1/4 cup chopped nuts (optional)

Combine all ingredients in a small bowl; mix well. Store in a container with a tight-fitting lid. Store in the refrigerator up to 1 week.

Vegetable Cream Cheese

8 ounces cream cheese, softened
1/2 cup finely chopped carrots, red bell pepper, radishes, celery, and scallions

Combine all ingredients in a small bowl; mix well. Store in a container with a tight-fitting lid. Store in the refrigerator up to 2 weeks.

Herb Cream Cheese

8 ounces cream cheese, softened
1/4 cup chopped fresh herbs (dill, chives, tarragon, basil, etc.) or 1 tablespoon dried herbs

Combine all ingredients in a small bowl; mix well. Store in a container with a tight-fitting lid. Store in the refrigerator up to 2 weeks.

Pineapple Cream Cheese

$1/2$ cup crushed pineapple, drained

8 ounces cream cheese, softened

Combine all ingredients in a small bowl; mix well. Store in a container with a tight-fitting lid. Store in the refrigerator up to 2 weeks.

Berry Cream Cheese

8 ounces cream cheese, softened

2 tablespoons fresh blueberries, strawberries, and raspberries, puréed

1 teaspoon sugar

Combine all ingredients in a small bowl; mix well. Store in a container with a tight-fitting lid. Store in the refrigerator up to 1 week.

Banana-Nut Cream Cheese

1 large ripe banana, mashed

$1/4$ cup walnuts, chopped

8 ounces cream cheese, softened

Combine all ingredients in a small bowl; mix well. Store in a container with a tight-fitting lid. Store in the refrigerator up to 1 week.

Serving Suggestions

Spread on:
- black bread
- onion rolls
- Pumpkin Bread (page 10), Banana Bread (page 9), or Whole Wheat Carrot-Walnut Bread (page 11)
- bagels, any variety
- Fruity Muffins (page 13)

PESTO DRESSINGS

Basil Pesto Dressing

2 cups tightly packed basil leaves

2 garlic cloves

1/2 cup pine nuts

1/3 cup grated Parmesan cheese (optional)

3/4 cup olive oil

salt and freshly ground black pepper,
     to taste

Tip

When it comes to pesto dressings, a little goes a long way. Spread on sandwiches or stir a dollop into a salad for a burst of fresh flavor. For a thinner dressing, add more oil or stock until desired consistency is reached. Adjust seasoning to taste.

1. Blend the basil, garlic, pine nuts, and cheese, if desired, in a food processor or blender.

2. Gradually add the olive oil in a thin, steady stream. Season with salt and pepper.

Makes about 1 cup

Sun-dried Tomato Pesto Dressing

2/3 cup sun-dried tomatoes packed in oil, drained

1/4 cup olive oil

1/4 cup grated Parmesan cheese

I small garlic clove

Combine all ingredients in a food processor or blender; process until finely chopped and blended.

Makes about 1/2 cup

Light Pesto Dressing

1/2 cup firmly packed basil leaves

1/4 cup chicken broth

1/4 cup grated Parmesan cheese

2 teaspoons olive oil

I small garlic clove

salt and freshly ground black pepper, to taste

Combine all the ingredients in a food processor or blender. Process until smooth.

Makes about 1/2 cup

SALAD DRESSINGS

Chutney Dressing

1/2 cup mango chutney

3 tablespoons white wine vinegar

1 1/2 teaspoons Dijon mustard

3/4 tablespoon soy sauce

1 1/2 teaspoons sesame oil

1/2 teaspoon crushed red pepper flakes

1 large garlic clove, chopped

salt and freshly ground black pepper, to taste

Combine all ingredients in a food processor or blender; purée until smooth.

Makes about 1/2 cup

Lemon-Mustard Dressing

3 tablespoons freshly squeezed lemon juice

1 tablespoon Dijon mustard

1 garlic clove, minced

1/2 teaspoon dried oregano, tarragon, or dill

1/3 cup olive oil

salt and freshly ground black pepper, to taste

Combine the lemon juice, mustard, garlic, and oregano in a small bowl. Whisk in the oil in a slow, steady stream until well blended. Season with salt and pepper.

Makes about 1/2 cup

Balsamic or Red Wine Vinaigrette

1 1/2 to 2 tablespoons balsamic vinegar or red wine vinegar

1/4 cup olive oil

1/2 teaspoon salt

freshly ground black pepper, to taste

Whisk all ingredients together in a small bowl until well combined.

Makes about 1/3 cup

Tahini Dressing

    4 tablespoons tahini

    3 tablespoons freshly squeezed lemon juice

    1 tablespoon soy sauce

    2 small garlic cloves, minced

    1/8 teaspoon crushed red pepper flakes

Whisk all ingredients together in a small bowl until well combined.

Makes about 1/3 cup   ·

Basic Vinaigrette

    2 tablespoons vinegar or citrus juice

    4 tablespoons olive oil

    salt and freshly ground black pepper, to taste

Whisk all ingredients in a small bowl; mix well. Now use your imagination and add Dijon mustard, honey, fresh herbs, cheese, garlic, or other flavorings.

Makes about 1/3 cup

Sweet Asian Dressing

    4 tablespoons vegetable oil

    1 tablespoon sesame oil

    3 tablespoons rice vinegar

    2 tablespoons soy sauce

    1 1/4 teaspoons sugar

    2 teaspoons finely grated ginger

Whisk all ingredients together in a small bowl until well combined.

Makes about 1/2 cup

Poppy Seed Dressing

1/4 cup cider vinegar

1/4 cup vegetable oil

1/4 cup honey

1/4 teaspoon Worcestershire sauce (optional)

1 teaspoon poppy seeds

Whisk all ingredients together in a small bowl until well combined.

Makes about 2/3 cup

Caesar Salad Dressing

1/2 cup olive oil

3 garlic cloves

3 tablespoons freshly squeezed lemon juice

2 teaspoons Dijon mustard

1 teaspoon Worcestershire sauce

3 anchovies, drained

1/2 cup freshly grated Parmesan cheese

Combine all ingredients together in a food processor or blender; blend well.

Makes about 1/2 cup

Timesaving Tips

- These salad dressings are used in recipes throughout the book. Bottled salad dressing can be substituted to save time.
- Instead of whisking all ingredients together in a bowl, combine all ingredients in a container with a tight-fitting lid and shake like mad until well blended. Refrigerate extra dressing up to 2 weeks.

LiGHT DRESSiNGS

Give up salad dressing because you are watching fat and calories? No way! With these easy homemade recipes you don't have to eat dry salad unless you want to (which can be very delicious when seasonal veggies are at their peak!).

Southwestern Dressing

  4 tablespoons olive or canola oil

  3 tablespoons freshly squeezed lime juice

  2 garlic cloves, minced

  I teaspoon ground cumin

  salt, to taste

  I to 2 tablespoons chopped fresh cilantro (optional)

Whisk all ingredients together in a small bowl until well combined.

Makes about ¹/₂ cup

Vegetable Juice Dressing

  ¹/₂ cup eight-vegetable juice

  2 tablespoons red wine vinegar

  ¹/₂ teaspoon Dijon mustard

  ¹/₂ teaspoon sugar

  ¹/₂ teaspoon prepared white horseradish

  salt and freshly ground black pepper, to taste

Whisk all ingredients together in a small bowl until well combined.

Makes about ¹/₂ cup

Calorie—Cutting Tips

- Use only enough dressing to coat the salad. Place salad in a self-sealing plastic bag, pour in the dressing, seal, and shake vigorously.
- Substitute nonfat yogurt for mayonnaise.
- Decrease the amount of oil in the recipe and add vinegar or citrus juice.

Dill-Yogurt Dressing

3 tablespoons fat-free mayonnaise
3 tablespoons nonfat plain yogurt
2 tablespoons chopped fresh dill
1 1/2 teaspoons Dijon mustard
1 1/2 teaspoons white wine vinegar
1 1/2 teaspoons prepared white horseradish
salt and freshly ground black pepper, to taste

Whisk all ingredients together in a small bowl until well combined.

Makes about 1/2 cup

FLAVORED MAYONNAISE

Turn ordinary into gourmet with these flavored mayonnaises. Flavored mayonnaise can be stored in a covered container in the refrigerator for up to 1 week.

Garlic Mayonnaise

1 teaspoon freshly squeezed lemon juice
1 teaspoon minced garlic
1/2 cup mayonnaise

Combine all ingredients in a small bowl; mix well.

Makes about 1/2 cup

Serving Suggestion

Spread liberally over your favorite sandwich filling for a fast gourmet sandwich.

Pesto Mayonnaise

1/4 cup any homemade Pesto Dressing (page 16)
1/4 cup mayonnaise

Combine all ingredients in a small bowl; mix well.

Makes about 1/2 cup

Dijon Mayonnaise

1 1/2 tablespoons Dijon mustard
2 tablespoons chopped fresh dill (optional)
1/2 cup mayonnaise

Combine all ingredients in a small bowl; mix well.

Makes about 1/2 cup

Chive Mayonnaise

1/2 cup mayonnaise
1/3 cup snipped fresh chives
2 small garlic cloves, minced
freshly ground black pepper, to taste

Combine all ingredients in a small bowl; mix well.

Makes about 1/2 cup

Sun-dried Tomato Mayonnaise

1 small clove garlic
1/4 cup chopped sun-dried tomatoes, packed in olive oil, well drained
1/2 cup mayonnaise

In a food processor or blender, combine the garlic and sun-dried tomatoes; process until finely chopped and smooth; transfer to a small bowl. Add mayonnaise to sun-dried tomato mixture; mix well.

Makes about 1/2 cup

Horseradish Mayonnaise

3 tablespoons prepared white horseradish
1/2 cup mayonnaise
1/2 teaspoon dried thyme (optional)
salt and freshly ground black pepper, to taste

Combine all ingredients in a small bowl; mix well.

Makes about 1/2 cup

Herb Mayonnaise

1/2 cup mayonnaise

2 1/2 tablespoons fresh chopped herbs of your choice (any combination of parsley, chives, dill, tarragon, oregano, thyme, and basil)

Combine all ingredients in a small bowl; mix well.

Makes about 1/2 cup

Dill Mayonnaise

1/2 cup mayonnaise

1/4 cup fresh dill, chopped

1 tablespoon freshly squeezed lemon juice

1 teaspoon minced garlic

salt and freshly ground black pepper to taste

Combine all ingredients in a small bowl; mix well.

Makes about 1/2 cup

Black Pepper Mayonnaise

1/2 cup mayonnaise

1 teaspoon freshly ground black pepper

1 teaspoon freshly squeezed lemon juice

Combine all ingredients in a small bowl; mix well.

Makes about 1/2 cup

Honey-Mustard Mayonnaise

1/2 cup mayonnaise

1 tablespoon freshly squeezed lime juice

1 tablespoon honey

1 tablespoon Dijon mustard (optional)

Combine all ingredients in a small bowl; mix well.

Makes about 1/2 cup

Cutting Tip

Calories!

Reduce the fat, cholesterol, and calories in your flavored mayonnaise by using cholesterol- and fat-free mayonnaise.

FLAVORED MUSTARD

Dijon mustard is a wonderful condiment that adds life to many sandwiches. Try enhancing its flavor with any of the following easy combinations. These mustards will keep in the refrigerator for a month.

Dill Mustard

1/2 cup Dijon mustard
2 tablespoons chopped fresh dill
freshly ground black pepper, to taste

Combine all ingredients in a small bowl; mix well.

Makes about 1/2 cup

Serving Suggestions

These mustards make terrific dipping sauces for pretzels, flat breads, chips, and vegetable sticks. And they have the added bonus of being low in fat and calories.

Horseradish Mustard

1/2 cup Dijon mustard
2 tablespoons prepared white horseradish, drained

Combine all ingredients in a small bowl; mix well.

Makes about 1/2 cup

Honey Mustard

1/2 cup Dijon mustard
2 1/2 tablespoons honey

Combine all ingredients in a small bowl; mix well.

Makes about 1/2 cup

Raspberry Mustard

1/2 cup Dijon mustard
3 tablespoons seedless raspberry preserves

Combine all ingredients in a small bowl; mix well.

Makes about 1/2 cup

Chapter Two

GOURMET SANDWICHES AND SOUPS

The simple sandwich wears many hats, from an effortless quick bite to an elegant, flavorful meal. With the variety of fillings, breads, and condiments, combinations are endless. Sandwiches have even found their way into menus of fine restaurants and gourmet take-out shops. But with fame comes a new name—gourmet sandwich—and a heavier price tag. These tasty beauties can cost as much as a moderately priced dinner entrée.

Fortunately, wonderful gourmet sandwiches can be prepared at home for about a quarter of the price of store bought. Think of your kitchen as a personal gourmet shop—experiment with new combinations and indulge your taste buds. The recipes in this chapter will give you inspiration and delicious results.

You will also find recipes at the end of this chapter for easy-to-make soups. A cup of soup and half a sandwich makes a wonderful lunch.

GRILLED EGGPLANT, ROASTED PEPPER, AND GOAT CHEESE SANDWICH

2 hero rolls, split in half
6 slices grilled eggplant (see Grilled Vegetables, page 3)
1 Roasted Pepper (page 4), cut into strips
3 ounces crumbled goat cheese
1/2 cup arugula, stems trimmed
2 to 4 tablespoons Balsamic or Red Wine Vinaigrette (page 17) or
    Basil Pesto Dressing (page 16)

1. Layer the bottom of the bread with eggplant slices, pepper strips, goat cheese, and arugula.

2. Sprinkle on Balsamic Vinaigrette. Gently close sandwiches; cut in half crosswise. Wrap tightly in aluminum foil

Makes 2 sandwiches

Pack Along

Raspberry Oatmeal Bars (page 100)

Variations

Add:
- Grilled Chicken (page 5)
- Sun-dried tomatoes (hydrated before adding)

Substitutes for goat cheese:
- mozzarella cheese
- feta cheese
- your personal favorite
- omit entirely for a grilled vegetable sandwich

SALAMI, PROVOLONE, AND ROASTED RED PEPPER SANDWICH

8 thin slices Italian-style salami
2 slices Provolone cheese
4 slices sourdough bread or brioche
1 Roasted Red Pepper (page 4), cut into strips
4 thin slices red onion
extra virgin olive oil or Balsamic Vinaigrette (page 17)
freshly ground black pepper

Variations

How about trying:
- salami and Swiss
- salami and feta
- salami and mozzarella

1. Layer the salami and Provolone evenly on two slices of bread. Top each bread evenly with the roasted pepper, and onion slices.

2. Drizzle olive oil over the onion slices. Season liberally with pepper.

3. Gently close sandwiches; cut in half crosswise. Wrap tightly in aluminum foil.

Makes 2 sandwiches

Pack Along
potato chips

CHICKEN SANDWICH WITH MANGO SLICES AND CHUTNEY DRESSING

Chutney Dressing (page 17)
2 slices multigrain rolls, split in half
2 Poached Chicken Breast halves (page 2)
4 red lettuce leaves
4 mango slices

1. Spread the Chutney Dressing on tops and bottoms of rolls.

2. Layer the chicken, lettuce, and mango slices on bottoms of rolls.

3. Gently close sandwiches; cut in half crosswise. Wrap tightly in aluminum foil.

Pack Along

Makes 2 sandwiches

**Flavored Popcorn
(page 111)**

Timesaving Tip

Make a batch of
Poached Chicken
Breasts (page 2) and
Grilled Vegetables
(page 3) on the week-
end. Lunch will be
a snap to prepare
all week long.

MEDITERRANEAN SANDWICH

A great sandwich for a picnic at the park or beach.

1 small loaf French bread
4 tablespoons olive oil
1/4 cup freshly squeezed lemon juice
1 large garlic clove, minced
2 ripe plum tomatoes, chopped
1 red bell pepper, chopped
1/4 cup chopped red onion
2 tablespoons chopped, pitted black olives
1 can (3 ounces) white-meat tuna
salt and freshly ground black pepper, to taste

Tip

For a terrific salad, add a can of drained cannelloni beans to the tuna mixture. Be sure to pack some crusty bread.

1. Cut the bread in half lengthwise; scoop out the insides to create a shell.

2. Drizzle 1 tablespoon of the oil over the bottom half of the bread.

3. Whisk together the lemon juice, remaining olive oil, and the garlic in a small bowl.

4. Add the tomatoes, pepper, onion, olives, tuna, salt, and pepper to lemon mixture; mix well.

5. Spoon into the bottom bread shell. Gently close sandwiches; cut in half crosswise. Wrap tightly in aluminum foil.

Makes 2 sandwiches

Pack Along

- a fresh fruit salad
- Dried Fruit Compote (page 102)

SUN-DRIED TOMATO CREAM CHEESE ON A BAGEL

4 sun-dried tomatoes (not packed in oil)
$^1/_2$ cup cream cheese, at room temperature
$^1/_4$ cup chopped black olives
2 bagels, split in half
6 arugula leaves, stems removed

1. Place the tomatoes in a small bowl and cover with boiling water. Set aside for 10 to 15 minutes. Drain; finely chop.

2. Place the cream cheese in a small bowl. Mix in the sun-dried tomatoes and olives.

3. Spread a layer of cream cheese mixture on two bagel halves. Top with arugula. Gently close sandwiches; cut in half crosswise. Wrap tightly in aluminum foil.

Variations

Top with:
- **Poached Chicken Breasts (page 2)**
- **ham slices**

Makes 2 sandwiches

Pack Along
- **Flavored Popcorn (page 111)**
- **fresh fruit**

GRILLED VEGETABLE AND RICOTTA SANDWICH

Ricotta salata is a tangy, creamy cheese. If you can't find it, use feta or goat cheese.

2 ounces ricotta salata cheese, crumbled
1 teaspoon freshly squeezed lemon juice
1 tablespoon fresh oregano, finely chopped
pinch of crushed red pepper flakes
salt and freshly ground black pepper, to taste
2 baguettes, split in half
1 cup assorted Grilled Vegetables (page 3),
    cut into strips
1/4 teaspoon olive oil

Pack Along

Low-Fat
Walnut–Chocolate
Chip Biscotti
(page 109)

1. Place the ricotta salata in a small bowl; mash. Add the lemon juice, oregano, pepper flakes, salt, and pepper; mix well.

2. Spread the mixture over the bottoms of the baguettes.

3. Cover cheese mixture with Grilled Vegetables. Drizzle with olive oil. Gently close sandwiches; cut in half crosswise. Wrap tightly in aluminum foil.

Tip

Ricotta salata is also wonderful when teamed with sun-dried tomatoes, roasted peppers, and one of the Pesto Dressings (page 16).

Makes 2 sandwiches

SMOKED HAM AND ROASTED PEPPERS ON PUMPKIN BREAD

¹/₄ pound Virginia ham, thinly sliced
4 slices Pumpkin Bread (page 10)
1 Roasted Pepper (page 4), thinly sliced
freshly ground black pepper, to taste
1 tablespoon olive oil

1. Layer ham evenly on two slices of Pumpkin Bread. Top with roasted pepper.

2. Season liberally with black pepper. Drizzle on olive oil.

3. Gently close sandwiches; cut in half crosswise. Wrap tightly in aluminum foil.

Makes 2 sandwiches

Pack Along

- a small tossed salad
- fresh fruit
- Oatmeal-Raisin Cookies (page 108)

Serving Suggestions

Curiously delicious sandwich combinations include:

- smoked salmon with Horseradish Mayonnaise (page 22) on black bread
- Poached Chicken Breasts (page 2) and apricot jam on Corn Bread (page 11) or Whole Wheat Carrot-Walnut Bread (page 10)
- Grilled Chicken (page 5) with shredded carrots, butter lettuce, and Honey Mustard (page 24) on whole wheat bread
- prosciutto and mozzarella with red pepper mayonnaise (variation of Black Pepper Mayonnaise, page 23) on baguette
- Poached Chicken Breasts (page 2), avocado, cheddar cheese, and Russian dressing on multi-grain bread or sourdough baguette
- smoked turkey, smoked Gouda cheese, mixed greens, and Black Pepper Mayonnaise (page 23) on baguette

THE BEST ROAST BEEF SANDWICH

4 slices black bread
2 to 4 tablespoons Horseradish Mayonnaise (page 22)
8 ounces cooked roast beef, thinly sliced
4 thin onion slices (red or Vidalia)
4 romaine lettuce leaves

1. Spread the Horseradish Mayonnaise on two slices of the bread.

2. Layer the roast beef, onion slices, and lettuce leaves evenly on the prepared bread.

3. Gently close sandwiches; cut in half crosswise. Wrap tightly in aluminum foil.

Tip

Experiment with other Flavored Mayonnaise (pages 21–23), cheese, and greens to create new combinations.

Makes 2 sandwiches

TURKEY SANDWICH

Simple, delicious, and slightly unusual with the addition of Black Pepper Mayonnaise. Top with your favorite cheese if desired.

6 ounces fresh turkey breast, thinly sliced
4 slices rye bread
4 romaine lettuce leaves
I small tomato, thinly sliced
2 to 4 tablespoons Black Pepper Mayonnaise (page 23)

1. Evenly layer the turkey on two slices of bread. Top with lettuce and tomato.

2. Spread the Black Pepper Mayonnaise on the remaining bread. Gently close sandwiches; cut in half crosswise. Wrap tightly in aluminum foil.

Pack Along

- chips
- Mocha Chip Brownies (page 98)

Makes 2 sandwiches

TANGY SHRIMP SANDWICH

1/4 pound cooked medium shrimp, cleaned, deveined, and cut in half
1 teaspoon mayonnaise
salt and freshly ground black pepper, to taste
2 tablespoons prepared barbecue sauce
2 kaiser rolls, cut in half
1/2 cup shredded cabbage

1. Combine the shrimp, mayonnaise, salt, and pepper in a small bowl. Toss to coat evenly.

2. Spread barbecue sauce on both halves of the rolls.

3. Cover the bottom halves with the shrimp mixture. Top with the cabbage. Gently close sandwiches; cut in half crosswise. Wrap tightly in aluminum foil.

Makes 2 sandwiches

ANTIPASTO SANDWICH

2 tablespoons Pesto Mayonnaise (page 21) or prepared Italian dressing
2 Italian hero rolls, split in half
1 plum tomato, sliced, or 4 small sun-dried tomatoes packed in oil, drained
4 small slices mozzarella cheese
1 Roasted Pepper (page 4, or prepared), cut into strips
1 jar (3 1/2 ounces) marinated artichoke hearts (1/2 cup), drained and quartered

1. Spread 1 tablespoon of Pesto Mayonnaise on the top halves of the heroes.

2. Layer the bottom halves of the rolls evenly with tomato slices, mozzarella cheese, pepper slices, and artichoke heart quarters.

3. Gently close sandwiches; cut in half crosswise. Wrap tightly in aluminum foil.

Variation

Add some Italian salami for a spicier version of this delicious cold antipasto on bread.

Makes 2 sandwiches

CHICKEN COBB SANDWICH

- 2 multi-grain rolls, split in half
- 2 Poached Chicken Breasts (page 2)
- 3 ounces blue cheese, crumbled
- 4 slices crisply cooked bacon, crumbled
- 2 romaine lettuce leaves
- 2 tablespoons Balsamic or Red Wine Vinaigrette (page 17) or Lemon-Mustard Dressing (page 24)

1. Layer each bottom half of the rolls with a chicken breast, half of the blue cheese, and half of the bacon. Top with lettuce.

2. Drizzle Balsamic or Red Wine Vinaigrette on top of the lettuce. Gently close sandwiches; cut crosswise. Wrap tightly in aluminum foil.

Pack Along

Strawberry-Chocolate Shortbread Bars (page 101)

Makes 2 sandwiches

AMERICAN-STYLE HERO

- 2 ounces roast beef, thinly sliced
- 2 ounces cooked turkey breast, thinly sliced
- 2 ounces ham, thinly sliced
- 2 ounces cheddar, American, or Swiss cheese, thinly sliced
- 1/4 cup grated lettuce
- 1/4 cup grated carrots
- 1 small tomato, thinly sliced
- 2 Italian hero rolls, split in half
- 4 tablespoons prepared Russian dressing or mayonnaise

1. Layer the roast beef, turkey, ham, cheese, lettuce, carrots, and tomato slices evenly over the bottom halves of the bread.

2. Spread the dressing over the top halves of the bread. Gently close sandwiches; cut in half crosswise. Wrap tightly in aluminum foil.

Makes 2 sandwiches

CHEESY VEGETABLE SANDWICH

4 slices multi-grain bread
4 slices Muenster cheese
1/2 small cucumber, thinly sliced
1/2 cup carrots, shredded
1/2 cup alfalfa sprouts
4 romaine lettuce leaves
4 thin tomato slices
2 to 4 tablespoons Herb Mayonnaise
   (page 23)

Pack Along

- a thermos of soup
- fresh fruit

1. Layer two slices of bread with Muenster cheese, cucumber slices, carrots, alfalfa sprouts, lettuce, and tomato slices.

2. Spread a thin layer of Herb Mayonnaise on the remaining bread. Gently close sandwiches; cut crosswise. Wrap in aluminum foil.

Makes 2 sandwiches

Tip

Personalize this sandwich with your favorite vegetables, cheese, and Flavored Mayonnaise (pages 21–23) or one of the Pesto Dressings (page 16).

Variations

Expand your taste for cheese. Substitute different varieties in salad and sandwich recipes throughout the book. You may come up with a new favorite combination!

- Jarlsberg cheese
- cheddar cheese
- Swiss cheese
- roquefort cheese
- goat cheese
- ricotta salata cheese
- gorgonzola cheese
- edam cheese

GAZPACHO

2 ripe tomatoes, chopped

1/2 medium cucumber, peeled and chopped

1 small onion, chopped

1/4 cup green bell pepper, chopped

1/4 cup red bell pepper, chopped

1 garlic clove, crushed

1/2 cup eight-vegetable juice

1/2 tablespoon olive oil

1/2 tablespoon red wine vinegar

dash of Tabasco sauce

salt and freshly ground black pepper, to taste

1. Combine all the ingredients in a food processor or blender. Pulse (short on/off bursts) until vegetables are coarsely chopped and mixture is combined, about four or five pulses. Refrigerate until cold, at least 1 hour.

2. Pack soup in a chilled wide-mouth thermos.

Serving Suggestion

Add some crusty bread or a small garden salad for a tasty low-fat meal.

Makes 2 to 3 servings

Variation

For a spicier version, add a few tablespoons of hot prepared Mexican salsa or a few more dashes of Tabasco sauce. Garnish with cubed avocado and a dollop of fat-free yogurt.

SPLIT PEA SOUP

2 cups split peas, picked over and rinsed
1 small onion, chopped
3 carrots, chopped
2 celery stalks, chopped
2 quarts water
1 teaspoon dried thyme
1 teaspoon salt
freshly ground black pepper, to taste

1. Place all the ingredients in a large pot.

2. Bring liquid to a boil, reduce heat, cover, and simmer for about 1 hour. Stir occasionally.

3. Transfer mixture to a food processor or blender; purée in batches. Adjust seasoning; place back in pot and heat through. Pack in a preheated thermos.

Serving Suggestion

Pack some crusty rye bread or multi-grain rolls and Low-Fat Carrot Squares (page 106) for dessert. Terrific on a cold wintry day.

Makes 6 to 8 servings

Variations

For a heartier soup, add any of the following and heat through before serving:
- sliced cooked frankfurters
- smoked turkey
- cooked ham

JULIE'S CHICKEN NOODLE SOUP

My dear friend, Julie Morowitz, suggests serving this wonderful chicken soup for lunch with half a tuna sandwich, or when anyone is feeling under the weather.

I chicken pullet (4 pounds), cut into quarters

I small onion, peeled

2 quarts water

3 carrots, cleaned and cut into I" chunks

2 celery stalks, cleaned and cut into I" chunks

I parsnip, peeled

I teaspoon salt

white pepper, to taste

8 sprigs fresh parsley, tied together

6 sprigs fresh dill, tied together

1/2 pound thin egg noodles, cooked

Variations

Substitute the following for the noodles:

• rice—for chicken and rice soup

• alphabet pasta—for alphabet chicken soup

1. Place the chicken, onion, and water in a large pot; cook over high heat until liquid boils, skimming off foam as it occurs.

Tip

The trick to delicious chicken soup is refrigerating the finished stock and removing the hardened chicken fat. Strain the stock and use it as a base for a variety of soups, dressings, and stews.

2. Add the remaining ingredients, except noodles. Bring liquid to a second boil. Reduce heat to low and continue cooking, partially covered, for 1 hour.

3. Remove the onion, parsley, and dill. Let soup cool to room temperature before storing in an airtight container. Refrigerate the stock at least 2 hours, or overnight, to allow the fat to accumulate on the surface. Remove the fat with a slotted spoon.

4. Return the stock to a large saucepan and warm over medium heat; adjust seasoning and add the noodles. Pack the soup in a preheated thermos.

Makes 6 to 8 servings

EASY MINESTRONE SOUP

This soup is a snap with the help of frozen and canned vegetables.

2 tablespoons olive oil

1 medium onion, finely chopped

3 garlic cloves, minced

6 cups Julie's Chicken Noodle Soup stock (page 39) or low-fat canned chicken broth

1 can (16 ounces) plum tomatoes, coarsely chopped, juices reserved

2 tablespoons tomato paste

1 package (16 ounces) mixed frozen vegetables, thawed and drained

2 teaspoons Italian seasoning

salt and freshly ground black pepper, to taste

1 can (16 ounces) red kidney beans, rinsed and drained

1/2 cup uncooked small macaroni, elbow, or Tubetti pasta

freshly grated Parmesan cheese, to garnish

Serving Suggestion

Pack half an Antipasto Sandwich (page 34) and Low-Fat Walnut–Chocolate Chip Biscotti (page 109).

1. Heat the oil in a large pot. Add the onion and garlic; cook over medium heat, until onions are translucent.

2. Add the stock, tomatoes, and tomato paste. Bring to a boil, reduce heat, and simmer for 15 minutes.

3. Add the vegetables, seasoning, salt, pepper, beans, and pasta. Simmer for 10 minutes. Adjust seasonings to taste.

4. Pack soup in a preheated thermos. Pack the Parmesan cheese separately; garnish at serving time.

Makes 6 to 8 servings

CREAM OF TOMATO SOUP

4 tablespoons unsalted butter
^{1}/2 cup chopped onion
^{1}/2 cup chopped celery
1 carrot, finely chopped
1 can (35 ounces) whole plum tomatoes, chopped; reserve juices
4 fresh basil leaves
salt and freshly ground black pepper, to taste
1 cup heavy cream
croutons (optional)

1. Melt the butter in a large pot over medium heat. Cook the onion, celery, and carrot, stirring occasionally, until onion is soft and translucent.

2. Add the tomatoes, basil, salt, and pepper. Cook for 15 minutes.

3. Purée the soup in batches in a food processor or blender. Return soup to the pot, stir in the cream, and warm through over low heat.

4. Pack soup in a preheated thermos. Pack croutons separately to garnish soup when serving.

Makes 6 to 8 servings

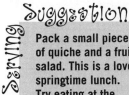
Serving Suggestion

Pack a small piece of quiche and a fruit salad. This is a lovely springtime lunch. Try eating at the neighborhood park or outside on the patio at work.

Chapter Three

SALADS

Salads are wonderful brown-bag fare. All preparation can be done in advance and they store well in plastic containers. As for ingredients and taste, you are only limited by your imagination and budget. With the cornucopia of fresh produce, pastas, grains, beans, cheeses, meats, poultry, and fish available, think of your salad bowl as a canvas and create your own masterpiece! Use fresh ingredients that complement each other in flavor and texture. Then pack some good-quality bread or crackers and you'll have a delicious lunch that pleases not only your tastebuds but also your healthy life-style.

The recipes in this chapter range from the traditional to the exotic. There is a delicious combination for every palate.

CHICKEN AND MIXED BERRY SALAD

2 cups torn red or green leaf lettuce or mixed greens

2 cups fresh mixed berries (blueberries, raspberries, sliced strawberries), washed

2 Poached Chicken Breasts (page 2), thinly sliced

Poppy Seed Dressing (page 19) or store-bought poppy seed dressing

1. Lightly toss the greens, berries, and chicken in a large bowl. Divide the salad evenly between plastic containers with tight-fitting lids.

2. Before serving, dress the salad and gently toss.

Makes 2 servings

Variation

Substitute melon cubes or orange sections for the mixed berries.

Pack Along

• Fruity Muffins (page 13)
• Banana Bread (page 9)

Tip

Most salads taste fresher if you pour the dressing on right before serving time. Pack dressing in a small, tightly covered plastic container.

SALMON-PASTA SALAD

1 cup uncooked pasta shells, elbows, or radiatore, cooked according to
    package directions
1/4 cup chopped red onion
1/2 cup frozen peas, thawed
8 ounces canned salmon, drained and flaked
1/2 cup Garlic Mayonnaise (page 21)
freshly ground black pepper, to taste

1. Place the pasta in a large bowl. Add the
onion, peas, and salmon; toss gently.

2. Pour the Garlic Mayonnaise on the
pasta; toss gently. Season with pepper.
Divide the salad evenly between plastic
containers with tight-fitting lids.

Pack Along

- **crackers**
- **Low-Fat Carrot Square (page 106)**

Makes 2 servings

Cutting Tip

Calories!

Make this salad low
calorie by substituting
fat-free garlic or Dijon
salad dressing for the
mayonnaise. Add some
fat-free flat breads for
the finishing touch.

Variations

Substitute for Garlic Mayonnaise:
- Pesto Mayonnaise (page 21)
- Dijon Mayonnaise (page 22)
Substitute canned tuna for the salmon.

SALADE NIÇOISE

2 small red potatoes

1/3 pound green beans, trimmed

2 small tomatoes, cut into quarters

1/4 cup chopped red onion

I can (7 ounces) tuna packed in oil or I can (7 1/2 ounces) salmon, drained and flaked

Lemon-Mustard Dressing (page 17)

1. Place the potatoes in a small saucepan; add salted water to cover. Bring the liquid to a boil, reduce heat to low, and simmer, covered, until the potatoes are just tender, about 10 minutes; drain. Transfer the potatoes to a plate; cool and slice.

2. Meanwhile, place the green beans in another small saucepan; add enough salted water to cover. Bring the liquid to a boil and cook until the beans are tender, about 5 minutes; drain and rinse under cold water. Transfer the beans to a large bowl.

Pack Along

- a baguette or black bread
- Orange Biscotti with Pine Nuts (page 104)

3. Add the potatoes, tomatoes, onion, and fish to the beans; toss gently.

4. Divide the salad evenly between plastic containers with tight-fitting lids.

5. Place the dressing in plastic containers with tight-fitting lids. Dress the salad at serving time; toss gently.

Makes 2 servings

Variations

For Salad Niçoise Sandwiches:
- Omit the potatoes and Lemon-Mustard Dressing.
- Mix tuna mixture with Dijon Mayonnaise (page 22).
- Serve on French bread.

LINGUINE AND BROCCOLI SALAD WITH SPICY PEANUT DRESSING

1 cup linguine, cooked according to
   package directions
1/2 cup broccoli florets, blanched (see Cooking
   Tip)
1/2 cup peanut butter
1 1/2 tablespoons soy sauce
1 1/2 tablespoons freshly squeezed lemon
   juice
1 garlic clove
3/4 teaspoon crushed red pepper flakes
1/2 teaspoon sugar
1/2 cup hot water or clear chicken broth
salt and freshly ground black pepper, to taste
1/4 cup chopped peanuts

Tip

Pasta and rice salads generally taste better when they marinate in the dressing.

Variations

Add:
- cubed marinated tofu
- your favorite vegetables
- leftover chicken or beef
- Grilled Vegetables (page 3)

Pack Along

- a multi-grain roll
- Raspberry-Oatmeal Bars (page 100)

1. Combine linguine and broccoli in a large bowl; set aside.

2. Place the remaining ingredients except peanuts in a food processor or blender; purée until smooth. Add the peanut butter mixture to the linguine mixture; toss to coat. Season with salt and pepper.

3. Divide the salad evenly between plastic containers with tight-fitting lids. Pack peanuts separately and garnish salad before serving.

Makes 2 servings

Cooking Tip

To blanch broccoli, place broccoli into boiling water until it turns bright green and is still crisp, about 1 minute. Quickly drain and rinse under cold water to stop cooking. Use the same method for snowpeas, only reduce cooking time by half.

CHICKEN WITH CURRY

2 Poached Chicken Breasts (page 2), sliced
1/2 cup diced ripe cantaloupe
1/4 cup chopped red onion
1 stalk celery, diced
1/4 cup raisins
1/2 cup Chutney Dressing (page 17)
1 teaspoon curry powder, or to taste
2 cups torn red leaf lettuce

1. Toss the chicken, cantaloupe, onion, celery, and raisins in a large bowl; mix well.

2. Combine the Chutney Dressing and the curry powder in a small bowl; mix well. Pour the chutney mixture over the chicken mixture; toss gently.

3. Divide the lettuce leaves equally between two plastic containers with tight-fitting lids. Divide the chicken salad between the containers and place on top of the lettuce.

Tip

For chutney in a flash: Mix a few tablespoons of cider vinegar with 1/2 cup peach jam.

Pack Along
- flat breads
- Lemon Bars (page 102)

Makes 2 servings

Variations

Add:
- toasted coconut
- chopped apples
- chopped seeded tomatoes
- chopped bacon
- cooked rice
- orange sections
- roasted peanuts

WALDORF SALAD

2 large apples, cored and diced
1 tablespoon freshly squeezed lemon juice
1 cup thinly sliced celery
1 cup curly endive or romaine lettuce, torn into pieces
1/4 cup raisins
1/4 cup chopped walnuts
2 tablespoons fat-free mayonnaise
2 tablespoons nonfat yogurt
2 teaspoons freshly squeezed lime juice
2 teaspoons honey

1. Place the apples in a large bowl and toss with the lemon juice.

2. Add the celery, endive, raisins, and chopped walnuts to the apples; toss to combine.

3. Mix the remaining ingredients together in a small bowl. Pour the mayonnaise mixture over the apple mixture; mix thoroughly until well coated.

4. Divide the salad evenly between plastic containers with tight-fitting lids.

Pack Along

**Whole Wheat
Carrot-Walnut Bread
(page 11)**

Makes 2 servings

Variations

Add:
• cooked chicken
• cooked turkey
• cooked ham
• cubed cheese
• chopped dates
• cubed pineapple

BOW TIES WITH GRILLED VEGETABLES

Simple to make when you have a batch of grilled vegetables on hand.

1 cup uncooked bow-tie pasta, cooked according to package directions
1/4 cup Balsamic or Red Wine Vinaigrette (page 17)
1 large garlic clove, minced
2 cups assorted Grilled Vegetables (page 3), cut into bite-size pieces
1 large Roasted Pepper (page 4), cut into bite-size pieces, about 1/2 cup
4 ounces goat, feta, or ricotta salata cheese, crumbled
1/4 cup fresh basil leaves, chopped
salt and freshly ground black pepper, to taste

Pack Along

Low-Fat Carrot Squares (page 106)

1. Combine the pasta, vinaigrette, and garlic in a large bowl; toss to combine.

2. Add the vegetables, cheese, and basil to the pasta mixture; toss gently. Season with salt and pepper.

3. Divide the salad evenly between plastic containers with tight-fitting lids.

Makes 2 servings

Money-saving Tip

Shells or elbow macaroni will also work well in this salad; both are less expensive than bow-tie pasta.

BEEF-PASTA SALAD IN ORANGE VINAIGRETTE

1/2 pound cooked beef, cut into strips (roast beef, London broil, strip, or flank steak work well)

I cup uncooked small tube, shell, or elbow pasta, cooked according to package directions

1/4 cup raisins

1/4 cup shredded carrots

I cup canned kidney beans, rinsed and drained

1/4 cup chopped chives or green onions

1/4 cup orange juice

I tablespoon grated orange zest*

I teaspoon cumin

1/4 cup store-bought red vinegar dressing or Basic Vinaigrette (page 18)

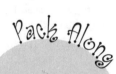

Pack Along

- pita breads or flour tortillas
- Dried Fruit Compote (page 102)

1. Combine the beef, pasta, raisins, carrots, beans, and chives in a large bowl; mix well.

2. Combine the orange juice, orange zest, cumin, and dressing in a small bowl; mix well. Pour the orange juice mixture over the beef mixture; toss to coat. Divide the salad evenly between plastic containers with tight-fitting lids.

Makes 2 servings

Tip

For an unusual sandwich, wrap this salad in flour tortillas. Kids will love these healthy packages. Just add a serving of milk and you'll be packing a lunch with something from all four food groups.

* The zest of the orange is the outermost peel without any of the pith (white membrane). To remove zest, use a zester or the fine side of a vegetable grater.

ASIAN TURKEY SALAD

Sweet Asian Dressing is usually a winner with the kids. Feel free to substitute their favorite vegetables.

1/2 medium cucumber, peeled, seeded, and cut into thin strips
1/2 cup thin strips of red bell pepper
1 cup coarsely chopped napa cabbage or red cabbage
4 to 6 ounces fresh cooked turkey, cut into thin strips
Sweet Asian Dressing (page 18)
1 tablespoon sesame seeds

1. Combine the cucumber, red bell pepper, cabbage, and turkey in a large bowl; toss well.

2. Pour the Sweet Asian Dressing over the salad; toss gently. Divide the salad evenly between plastic containers with tight-fitting lids. Pack sesame seeds separately; garnish before serving.

Variation

Add pasta and crisp Chinese noodles for an interesting pasta salad.

Makes 2 servings

Tip
This salad tastes better as it marinates.

Pack Along

- pita bread
- canned pineapple chunks

TORTELLINI SALAD WITH OLIVES AND FETA CHEESE

1 package (12 ounces) frozen cheese tortellini, cooked according to
   package directions
1 small tomato, chopped
1/4 cup red onion, chopped
1/2 cup black olives, chopped
1/2 cup crumbled feta cheese
Balsamic or Red Wine Vinaigrette (page 17)
   or prepared Italian dressing
1/2 cup walnuts, chopped (optional)

1. Combine all the ingredients except the dressing and nuts in a large bowl; mix well.

2. Add the dressing to the pasta mixture; toss gently. Divide the salad evenly between plastic containers with tight-fitting lids. Refrigerate overnight. Pack the nuts separately; garnish before serving.

Pack Along

• flat breads
• fresh fruit

Makes 2 servings

Timesaving Tip

Make a double batch of this salad. It refrigerates well and is a good side dish for a fish dinner.

ESTY'S STRING BEAN-WALNUT SALAD

It is always a treat when my mother, Esty Moskowitz, makes her "vegetarian chopped liver" salad. It is the same color and consistency of traditional chopped liver without all the fat and cholesterol of liver. Leftovers are terrific on onion crackers.

2 tablespoons olive oil
2 medium onions, finely chopped
4 hard-boiled eggs
1 can (14 ounces) cut string beans, drained
1 cup walnuts, finely chopped
$1/2$ cup plain bread crumbs
salt and freshly ground black pepper, to taste
$1/4$ teaspoon garlic powder
1 cup romaine lettuce, torn into pieces
6 cherry tomatoes, halved

Serving Suggestion

Try this uncommon salad on black bread; omit the cherry tomatoes and top with thin red onion and tomato slices.

1. Heat the olive oil in a small frying pan. Add the onions and cook over medium heat until golden brown, about 6 to 8 minutes. Remove from the heat.

Pack Along

- black bread
- Raspberry-Oatmeal Bars (page 100)

2. Place the onions, eggs, and string beans in a food processor; pulse (short on/off bursts) until finely chopped. Transfer to a large bowl.

3. Add the remaining ingredients, except the lettuce and tomatoes, to the bowl and mix thoroughly. If mixture is dry, add a few drops of olive oil.

4. Divide the lettuce evenly among plastic containers with tight-fitting lids. Pack the salad on top of the lettuce, and top with tomatoes.

Makes 3 servings

PASTA PRIMAVERA SALAD WITH CHEDDAR CHEESE

1 cup fettuccine, cooked according to package directions
1 small zucchini, cut into thin strips
1 yellow or red bell pepper, cut into thin strips
1/2 cup broccoli florets, blanched (page 46)
4 cherry tomatoes, halved
1/2 cup cheddar cheese, cubed
2 cups curly endive, torn into pieces
1/4 to 1/3 cup prepared creamy Italian salad
   dressing
Freshly ground black pepper, to taste

Variations

Add 1 cup:
• cooked chicken
• cooked beef

1. Combine the pasta, zucchini, bell pepper, broccoli, tomatoes, cheese, and endive in a large bowl; mix gently.

2. Add the dressing to the vegetable mixture; toss to coat. Season with pepper. Divide the salad evenly between plastic containers with tight-fitting lids.

Makes 2 servings

TORTELLINI SALAD WITH SUN-DRIED TOMATO PESTO

8 ounces cheese tortellini, cooked according to package directions
1/2 cup cubed mozzarella cheese
2 small tomatoes, quartered
3 to 4 tablespoons Sun-dried Tomato Pesto Dressing (page 16)
1 tablespoon balsamic vinegar
1/2 cup mixed salad greens

1. Combine the tortellini, cheese, tomatoes, dressing, and vinegar in a large bowl; toss to coat evenly.

2. Divide greens evenly between plastic containers with tight-fitting lids; top greens with pasta salad.

Makes 2 servings

TUNA-ARTICHOKE PASTA SALAD

1 jar (6½ ounces) marinated artichoke hearts (about ⅔ cup), drained and quartered

1 can (7½ ounces) tuna, drained and flaked

¼ cup chopped green onions

1 cup uncooked spiral pasta (radiatore), cooked according to package directions

¼ cup Balsamic or Red Wine Vinaigrette (page 17)

¼ tablespoon Dijon mustard

salt and freshly ground black pepper, to taste

1. Combine the artichokes, tuna, green onions, and pasta in a large bowl; toss well.

2. Whisk together the dressing and mustard in a small bowl. Add the dressing mixture to the pasta mixture; toss to coat. Season with salt and pepper.

3. Divide the salad evenly between plastic containers with tight-fitting lids.

Timesaving tip

This salad comes together quickly if you substitute a store-bought vinaigrette for the Balsamic Vinaigrette.

Makes 2 servings

Pack Along

- thick slice of Italian bread or a baguette
- Orange Biscotti with Pine Nuts (page 104)

APPLE, WALNUT, AND BLUE CHEESE SALAD

2 apples, cored and diced
1 teaspoon freshly squeezed lemon juice
1 cup radicchio, chicory, or Belgian endive leaves
1 cup romaine leaves, torn into bite-size pieces
2 green onions, chopped
1/2 cup walnut halves
3 ounces blue cheese, crumbled
1/4 cup Balsamic or Red Wine Vinaigrette (page 17) or store-bought red wine vinaigrette

1. Combine the apples and lemon juice in a small bowl; toss to coat. Set aside.

2. Combine the radicchio, romaine, and green onions in a bowl; toss to combine. Add the apples, walnuts, and cheese to the salad greens mixture; toss gently.

3. Divide the salad evenly between plastic containers with tight-fitting lids. Pack the dressing separately. Add dressing before serving; toss lightly to coat.

Variations

Add:
• **Poached Chicken Breasts (page 2)**
• **canned tuna**
• **cooked pasta**

Pack Along

• **multi-grain rolls or black bread**
• **White Chocolate Chip Cookies (page 97)**

Makes 2 servings

iF YOU HAVE A MICROWAVE

There is nothing like a hot lunch. It is comforting, satisfying, and with the help of a microwave, it can be prepared quickly and easily. The recipes in this chapter are simple and delicious. Try them—you'll appreciate a hot lunch every once in a while.

THE NO-MICROWAVE BLUES

True, it is more difficult to prepare and transport a hot brown-bag lunch without the help of a microwave. But don't be dismayed. With a little extra effort it can be successfully done. Follow the tips on pages 61 and 64 for packing hot food.

QUESADILLAS

1/2 cup canned refried beans or black bean dip
4 flour tortillas
1 Roasted Pepper (page 4), chopped
1/2 cup Grilled Vegetables (page 3), chopped,
   or shredded cooked chicken
2/3 cup shredded low-fat cheddar cheese
1 teaspoon chopped jalapeño pepper
   (optional)

Moneysaving tip

Quesadillas are a good way to use up small amounts of leftovers.

1. Spread 2 tablespoons of refried beans on one side of each flour tortilla.

2. Combine the Roasted Pepper and Grilled Vegetables in a small bowl; mix well. Spoon mixture evenly over refried beans.

3. Sprinkle cheese and jalapeño pepper evenly over vegetable mixture. Fold the tortilla in half over filling. Secure with a toothpick. Divide and pack in microwavable containers with tight-fitting lids.

Tip

Flour tortillas are a versatile and low-calorie way to wrap many sandwich fillings. Try wrapping up your favorite fillings for a delicious change.

Pack Along

- a small container of salsa
- Baked Tortilla Chips (page 110)
- Mocha Chip Brownies (page 98)

4. Before serving, microwave at High until the cheese has melted, 1 to 2 minutes. Cut in half and serve.

Makes 2 servings

Variations

Try these combinations:

- fresh mozzarella, chopped tomatoes, fresh basil, and olive oil
- finely chopped chicken, chopped red onion, tomato, black beans, olive oil, and freshly squeezed lemon juice

CHICKEN AND BEAN STEW

2 tablespoons olive oil

I small onion, chopped

2 garlic cloves, chopped

1/2 of a red bell pepper, chopped

I can (15 ounces) crushed tomatoes

2 tablespoons balsamic vinegar

1/2 teaspoon dried basil

salt, to taste

pinch of crushed red pepper flakes

I can (16 ounces) red kidney beans, drained
    and rinsed

3/4 pound cooked chicken, cubed

1/4 cup grated Parmesan cheese (optional)

Pack Along

- crusty, thick bread
- S'more Brownies (page 99)

1. Heat the oil in a large skillet. Add the onion, garlic, and bell pepper; cook over medium heat until the onion is translucent, about 7 minutes.

2. Add the tomatoes, vinegar, basil, salt, red pepper flakes, and beans; continue cooking, stirring frequently, 20 minutes. Add the chicken; cook until heated through, 5 minutes.

3. Pack the stew in microwavable plastic containers. Pack cheese separately. Before serving, microwave at High until heated through, 3 minutes. Top with grated cheese.

Microwave Method: Cook the oil, onion, garlic, and bell pepper in a large covered microwavable bowl at High 2 minutes. Stir. Continue cooking at High 3 minutes, until onion is translucent. Mix in the tomatoes, vinegar, basil, salt, pepper flakes, and beans. Cook at High, covered, 5 minutes. Add the chicken; cook an additional 5 minutes. Resume with step 3.

Makes 4 servings

CHEDDAR AND TOMATO QUICHE

1 1/2 cups half-and-half
3 large eggs
1 teaspoon Dijon mustard
salt and freshly ground black pepper, to taste
1 cup shredded cheddar cheese
1 cup chopped tomatoes
One 10-inch frozen prebaked pie shell or 6 individual shells

1. Preheat the oven to 350°F.

2. Combine the half-and-half, eggs, mustard, salt, and pepper in a bowl; whisk well.

3. Stir the cheese and tomatoes into the egg mixture.

- a thermos of soup
- slice of Whole Wheat Carrot-Walnut Bread (page 11)

4. Pour the egg mixture into the pie shell. Bake until set, about 40 minutes.

5. Pack the quiche in a microwavable dish. Before serving, microwave at High to heat through, 1 to 2 minutes.

Makes 6 to 8 servings

Variations

You can create a variety of quiches using the basic egg-and-cream custard in the recipe plus 1 to 2 cups of filling. Try some of the following combinations or create your own:

- Ratatouille (page 6) and Parmesan cheese
- broccoli and cheddar cheese
- spinach and feta cheese
- smoked salmon, fresh dill, sautéed onions, and mushrooms
- Swiss cheese, garlic, and sautéed mushrooms
- diced apples and cheddar cheese
- chopped ham and Swiss cheese

These savory pies can be frozen for up to 2 months. Add a small tossed salad to round out the meal.

CHILI IN A FLASH

1 medium onion, chopped
1 green bell pepper, chopped
1 pound lean ground beef or turkey
2 tablespoons chili powder
1 canned pickled jalapeño pepper, chopped (optional)
2 cans (14 ounces each) Mexican-style stewed tomatoes
1 can (16 ounces) kidney beans
1 cup shredded cheddar cheese

Tip

You can pack hot stews in a wide-mouth, preheated thermos if you don't have a microwave available.

1. Cook the onion, green bell pepper, and ground beef in a large skillet over medium heat until the beef is no longer pink, 6 minutes. Drain off the fat.

Suggestions

Serving

Chili is wonderful as:
- a stuffing for baked potatoes
- mixed with cooked pasta
- a dip with tortilla chips

2. Add the chili powder, jalapeño pepper, stewed tomatoes, and kidney beans; continue cooking, 20 minutes.

3. Pack the chili in microwavable plastic containers with tight-fitting lids. Pack the cheese separately. Before serving, microwave at High until heated through, 2 minutes. Garnish with cheddar cheese.

Pack Along

- Corn Bread (page 12)
- Baked Tortilla Chips (page 110)

Microwave Method: Cook onion, bell pepper, and beef in a microwavable dish at High until beef is no longer pink, 6 minutes. Drain off fat. Add chili powder and jalapeño; cook at High 1 minute. Add tomatoes and beans; cook at High about 7 minutes. Mix well. Resume with step 3.

Makes 4 servings

TURKEY AND SWISS MELT

4 ounces sliced smoked or plain turkey breast

2 slices Swiss cheese

4 tablespoons Russian dressing

4 slices rye or black bread

1. Pack the turkey topped with Swiss cheese in a microwavable container with a tight-fitting lid.

2. Pack the dressing and bread in separate containers.

3. Before serving, microwave the turkey and cheese at High until the cheese melts and turkey is warm, 3 minutes.

4. Spread a thin layer of dressing on two slices of bread. Top with the turkey and cheese. Gently close sandwich; cut in half crosswise.

Pack Along

- a pickle— in a plastic container with a tight-fitting lid
- chips

Variations

Makes 2 sandwiches

Add some:

- tart apple slices
- cooked bacon
- thin tomato slices

Make a Classic Reuben: Substitute corned beef and canned sauerkraut for the turkey and Russian dressing.

STUFFED POTATOES WITH TUNA AND CHEDDAR CHEESE

1 1/2 cups Tuna Salad (page 7)
1/2 cup shredded cheddar cheese
1/4 cup finely chopped apple, optional
2 medium-size potatoes, cooked

1. Combine the Tuna Salad, cheese, and apple in a small bowl; mix well. Pack tuna mixture in plastic containers with tight-fitting lids. Pack potatoes separately.

2. Before serving, microwave the potatoes until warm, 1 minute. Cut a lengthwise slit on top of each potato. Fluff the insides of the potato with a fork; top with the tuna mixture. Microwave at High or until potatoes are hot and cheese is slightly melted, 2 minutes.

Timesaving Tip

Pack a raw potato. Cook the potato in the microwave before serving.

Pack Along

Makes 2 servings

- tossed salad
- Spicy Apple Squares (page 107)

Variations

Try any of the following stuffings for a filling lunch. Use low-fat cheese if you are counting calories.

- chopped broccoli and cheddar cheese
- bacon, chopped tomato, and cheddar cheese
- chopped spinach and Swiss cheese
- chopped ham and Gruyère
- Ratatouille (page 6) and Parmesan cheese
- Mexican salsa, refried beans, and cheddar cheese
- Chili in a Flash (page 61)

STEAMED VEGETABLES AND TAHINI DRESSING

1 cup broccoli florets
1 large carrot, sliced into 1/4" rounds (1 cup)
1 small yellow zucchini, cut into 1/4" rounds (1 cup)
1/2 cup sugar snap peas, ends trimmed
1 small red or yellow bell pepper, cut into
    1" square strips (1/2 cup)
1/3 cup Tahini Dressing (page 18)

1. Combine all ingredients, except dressing, in a large bowl; mix well.

2. Pack vegetable mixture in microwavable containers with tight-fitting lids. Pack the dressing in two small plastic containers with tight-fitting lids.

Tip

If you do not have a microwave at your disposal steam the vegetables at home. Pack in a preheated thermos or eat at room temperature.

3. Before serving, sprinkle water on vegetables and cover tightly. Cook at High for 4 minutes or until done to desired tenderness. Pour on dressing; toss to combine.

Pack Along

Makes 2 servings

* pita rounds
* fresh fruit

Variations

Add:

* grilled lamb or steak strips
* sautéed vegetables
* grilled eggplant (see Grilled Vegetables, page 3)
* chopped Calamata olives
* falafel
* thinly sliced avocado
* tofu slices

CREAMY CHICKEN AND RAISIN ROLLS

Feel free to omit the chicken for a delicious vegetarian meal.

1/4 cup Raisin Cream Cheese (page 14) with walnuts, softened

2 tablespoons crushed pineapple, with juice

2 tablespoons shredded carrot

3/4 cup cooked chicken breasts or Poached Chicken Breasts (page 2), shredded

1 tablespoon shredded coconut

1/4 cup peeled, chopped apple

2 flour tortillas

Variation

Use your favorite sweet Flavored Cream Cheese (pages 14–15) and some dried fruit as a substitute for Raisin Cream Cheese. The recipe will take on a new taste.

1. Combine the cream cheese and pineapple in a small bowl; mix well.

2. Add the carrot, chicken, coconut, and apple; mix gently. Place half the filling into each tortilla; roll up. Pack tortillas, seam side down, in microwavable plastic containers with tight-fitting lids.

3. Before serving, microwave at High, uncovered, until heated through, 2 minutes.

Makes 2 servings

Pack Along

Flavored Popcorn (page 111)

Chapter Five

IT'S DIET TIME

It's hard to stick to a diet. Eating out makes it even harder. Packing a light brown-bag lunch keeps you away from the local coffee shop, take-out place, or fast food restaurant. Where there are lots of high-calorie foods lurking, making your lunch delicious and satisfying keeps you away from afternoon snacking. Whether it's five, ten, or fifty pounds you are trying to lose, bringing a brown-bag lunch gives you control of the menu, ingredients, and portions. And we all know that every little bit counts when you are on a diet.

The recipes in this chapter are considered light—250 to 350 calories per serving—low in fat, and, most important, delicious. Just because you are on a diet does not mean you have to eat carrot sticks and cottage cheese for lunch. And if you have room, you can even have a sensible dessert!

CALORIE-CUTTING TIPS

Many of the recipes throughout the book can be modified to fit into any low-fat, low-calorie diet. These ideas will help you lighten other recipes:

- use fat-free dressings
- use light condiments
- use nonfat cheeses
- use low-fat meats
- use smaller portions of protein and larger portions of vegetables
- use light breads

CHICKEN WITH MANGO SALSA

1 ripe medium-size mango, peeled, pitted, and diced (about 1 cup)

3 green onions, chopped

3 tablespoons diced red bell pepper

3 tablespoons chopped fresh cilantro or 1 teaspoon dried

1 to 2 teaspoons seeded and chopped fresh jalapeño pepper

1 1/2 tablespoons white wine vinegar

1 teaspoon olive oil

salt and freshly ground black pepper, to taste

2 small Poached Chicken Breasts (page 2), cut into strips

1 cup torn romaine lettuce leaves, washed

1. Combine all the ingredients, except the chicken and lettuce, in a large bowl; mix well.

2. Pack the lettuce in plastic containers with tight-fitting lids. Top lettuce with the chicken strips and mango salsa.

Pack Along

fat-free flat breads

Makes 2 servings

Variations

Substitutes for chicken:

• nonfat cottage cheese—for a refreshing twist to a typical diet meal

• 1/2 cup of cooked pasta rotelles

• black beans and corn

Tip

When selecting a mango, look for one with a skin ranging in color from yellow to orange-red, with touches of green. The fruit will give a little when you gently squeeze it. Mangoes will ripen at room temperature in a partially closed paper bag. Check on the ripeness daily.

VEGETABLE-PASTA SALAD

1/2 cup plain nonfat yogurt

1/2 tablespoon red wine vinegar, shallot vinegar, balsamic vinegar, or tarragon vinegar

1/2 teaspoon prepared white horseradish

1/2 teaspoon minced garlic

salt and freshly ground black pepper, to taste

pinch of dried herb (oregano, tarragon, dill)

3 cherry tomatoes, halved

1/4 cup thin strips of red or yellow bell pepper

1/4 cup broccoli florets, blanched (page 46)

2 tablespoons chopped red onion

I cup uncooked medium-size pasta shells, raditore, or penne, cooked according to package directions

I cup romaine lettuce, torn into pieces

Variations

Add:
- flaked tuna
- cooked shrimp
- Poached Chicken Breasts (page 2)

1. Combine the yogurt, vinegar, horseradish, garlic, salt, black pepper, and herb in a large bowl; mix well.

Pack Along

- slice of reduced-calorie bread
- Low-Fat Walnut–Chocolate Chip Biscotti (page 109)

2. Add the tomatoes, bell pepper, broccoli, onion, and pasta; mix gently.

3. Pack the lettuce in plastic containers with tight-fitting lids; top the lettuce with half of the pasta mixture.

Makes 2 servings

Tip

Who said pasta is fattening? The trick to preparing a low-calorie pasta lunch is keeping pasta portions to about 1/2 cup and using low-fat or low-calorie dressings and sauces.

BAKED EGGPLANT

olive oil cooking spray

2 tablespoons soy sauce or fat-free Italian salad dressing

1 teaspoon olive oil

1 garlic clove, minced

1 small eggplant, cut into $1/2$" rounds

salt and freshly ground black pepper, to taste

1. Preheat oven to 350° F. Spray a large baking sheet with cooking spray.

2. Combine the soy sauce with the olive oil and garlic in a small bowl; mix well. Place the eggplant on the baking sheet. Brush dressing mixture on both sides of the eggplant slices. Season with salt and pepper.

3. Bake the eggplant, basting with dressing mixture after 10 minutes, until tender, about 25 minutes.

4. Pack the eggplant in plastic containers with tight-fitting lids.

Tip

Eggplant soaks up liquids like a sponge so you may need to use some additional cooking spray during baking.

Makes 2 servings

Cutting Tip

Use Baked Eggplant as a substitute for grilled eggplant (see Grilled Vegetables, page 3) in any recipe.

Serving Suggestions

Baked eggplant is very versatile. Here are some low-calorie ideas:

- Add roasted peppers, sun-dried tomatoes (not packed in oil), and a sprinkle of Parmesan cheese. Mound on lettuce.
- Add to cooked pasta and vegetables.
- Layer with tomatoes and low-fat cheese on reduced-calorie bread. Microwave 1 minute until the cheese melts.

TABBOULEH

This is a favorite Middle Eastern dish. It makes a delicious and unusual lunch for less than 300 calories.

¹/₂ cup bulgur (available in health food stores and some supermarkets)
³/₄ cup diced and seeded tomatoes
¹/₄ cup chopped red onion
¹/₂ cup diced cucumber
¹/₄ cup diced green bell pepper
¹/₄ cup finely chopped fresh parsley
¹/₄ cup finely chopped fresh mint
1 tablespoon freshly squeezed lemon juice
1 tablespoon olive oil
1 small garlic clove, minced
salt and freshly ground pepper, to taste
2 cups romaine lettuce, torn into pieces

Pack Along

- pita bread
- Dried Fruit Compote (page 102)

1. Place the bulgur in a large bowl and cover with boiling water; let stand 20 minutes. Drain well and return it to the bowl.

2. Add the tomatoes, onion, cucumber, and bell pepper to the bulgur; toss well.

3. Combine the parsley, mint, lemon juice, oil, garlic, salt, and black pepper in a small bowl; mix well. Pour the dressing over the bulgur mixture; stir to combine evenly.

4. Pack the lettuce into plastic containers with tight-fitting lids; top the lettuce with the tabbouleh.

Variations

- Add crumbled goat cheese or feta cheese for some zip.
- Substitute fresh mixed berries for the tomatoes and garlic.
- Stuff into scooped-out tomatoes.

Makes 2 servings

PESTO PASTA SALAD

This is a wonderful lunch at about 350 calories.

$^1/_2$ cup grilled onion slices (see Grilled Vegetables, page 3), coarsely chopped

$^1/_2$ cup frozen peas, thawed

$^1/_2$ cup chopped and seeded tomato

$^3/_4$ cup uncooked small pasta shells, penne, or orzo, cooked according to package directions

Light Pesto Dressing (page 16)

salt and freshly ground black pepper, to taste

2 cups romaine lettuce, torn into bite-size pieces

Pack Along

- **fat-free bread sticks**
- **Low-Fat Walnut–Chocolate Chip Biscotti (page 109)**

1. Combine the grilled onion, peas, tomatoes, and pasta in a large bowl; mix well.

2. Pour the Light Pesto Dressing over the pasta mixture; toss gently. Season with salt and pepper.

3. Pack the lettuce into plastic containers with tight-fitting lids; top the lettuce with the pasta salad.

Makes 2 servings

Variation

Add some Poached Chicken Breasts (page 2) or cooked shrimp—and about 100 calories per serving.

BROWN RICE, BLACK BEAN, AND CORN SALAD

Kids will enjoy stuffing taco shells with this salad.

1 cup cooked brown rice

1/2 cup canned black beans, drained and rinsed

1/2 cup canned whole kernel corn or cooked fresh corn kernels

1/4 cup chopped red or yellow bell pepper

1 green onion, chopped

1/2 cup chopped and seeded tomato

2 tablespoons chopped fresh cilantro

1 ounce goat, feta, or ricotta salata cheese, crumbled (optional)

1/4 cup Southwestern Dressing (page 20)

2 cups torn mixed greens

Pack Along

- **Mexican salsa**
- **small portion (about ten) of Baked Tortilla Chips (page 110) or two taco shells**

1. Combine all ingredients, except dressing and lettuce, in a mixing bowl; toss gently.

2. Pour dressing over the mixture; toss again gently.

3. Pack lettuce into plastic containers with tight-fitting lids; top lettuce with salad.

Makes 2 servings

EASY CHICKEN AND SALSA SALAD

3 cups napa cabbage or red cabbage, thinly sliced
1/2 cup shredded carrot
1/2 cup thin strips cucumber
4 ounces cooked chicken, cut into thin strips
3/4 cup salsa
1 tablespoon chopped fresh cilantro

1. Combine the cabbage, carrot, cucumber, and chicken in a large bowl; toss well.

2. Add the salsa to the cabbage mixture; mix well to coat. Pack in plastic containers with tight-fitting lids. Garnish with chopped cilantro.

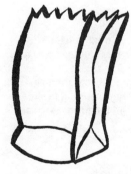

Serving Suggestion

Mound the salad on 1/2 cup of cold cooked rice. Surround with a few mango or melon slices. The entire lunch is about 300 calories.

Makes 2 servings

Tip

Test-taste different salsas with the kids. Choose a favorite and the entire family will be satisfied with this lunch.

Calorie-Cutting Tip

Salsa is a tasty addition to many salads and sandwiches. Add a spoon to rice, pasta, salads, or stews. You will have lots of taste for very few calories and (in most cases) no fat.

SALMON-CUCUMBER SALAD IN DILL-YOGURT DRESSING

1 can (7¹/₂ ounces) red or pink salmon, flaked
1 small seedless cucumber, peeled and thinly sliced
¹/₄ cup chopped green onion, white part only
¹/₄ cup chopped carrot
Dill-Yogurt Dressing (page 21)
salt and freshly ground black pepper, to taste
2 cups torn red lettuce leaves

Serving Suggestion

Mound on a hard roll or stuff into pita breads.

1. Combine the salmon, cucumber, green onion, and carrot in a large bowl; mix well.

2. Pour the dressing over the salad; mix to coat. Season to taste with salt and pepper.

3. Pack the lettuce into plastic containers with tight-fitting lids; top the lettuce with the salad.

Makes 2 servings

Pack Along

- rye crisps
- fresh fruit

Cutting Tip

Calories

If you want to lighten this meal further, prepare the Dill-Yogurt Dressing (page 21) substituting 3 tablespoons of fat-free yogurt for the mayonnaise.

Variations

Substitute for canned salmon:
- poached salmon
- canned or fresh cooked tuna
- cooked pasta, potatoes, or rice

COLD SESAME NOODLES WITH BROCCOLI AND ROASTED PEPPERS

2/3 cup diced Roasted Peppers (page 4)

2/3 cup frozen broccoli florets, thawed; or fresh florets, blanched (page 46)

3 green onions, finely chopped

3/4 cup uncooked linguine or spaghetti, cooked according to package directions

Tahini Dressing (page 18)

1. Combine the peppers, broccoli, onions, and pasta in a large bowl; toss well.

2. Pour the dressing on the salad; toss well. Pack salad in plastic containers with tight-fitting lids.

Pack Along

slice of reduced-calorie multi-grain bread or a pita round

Makes 2 servings

GUILTLESS SANDWICH

Are you trying to cut down on bread but miss biting into a sandwich? Here's your answer: the Lettuce Sandwich.

2 large romaine lettuce leaves

I cup Tuna Salad (page 7), Egg Salad (page 8), Chicken Salad (page 8), diced Poached Chicken Breasts (page 2), or 4 ounces assorted low-fat cold cuts

1. Pack the lettuce in self-sealing plastic bags. Pack the filling of choice in plastic containers with tight-fitting lids.

2. Before serving, place half the filling into the center of the lettuce leaf; roll up.

Makes 2 servings

FAJITA PASTA SALAD

1 cup uncooked orzo or small shelled pasta, cooked according to
    package directions
1 cup small pieces grilled onion (see Grilled Vegetables, page 3)
1 Roasted Pepper (page 4), cut into thin strips
2 small tomatoes, finely chopped
1 small jalapeño pepper, seeded and minced
1 Poached Chicken Breast (page 2), chopped
1/4 cup freshly squeezed lime juice
2 tablespoons olive oil
1 garlic clove, minced
salt and freshly ground black pepper, to taste
dash of hot red pepper sauce

Pack Along

• **container of salsa**
• **small portion (about ten) of Baked Tortilla Chips (page 110)**

1. Combine the pasta, onion, Roasted Pepper, tomatoes, jalapeño pepper, and chicken in a large bowl; mix well.

2. Combine the remaining ingredients together in a small bowl; whisk well. Pour dressing on the salad; mix to coat. Pack in plastic containers with tight-fitting lids.

Makes 2 servings

SHRIMP GAZPACHO SALAD

1/2 cup cooked shrimp, chopped
1 large cucumber, thinly sliced
2 medium tomatoes, chopped
1 carrot, thinly sliced
1 small red onion, thinly sliced
1 small green bell pepper, chopped
2 to 4 tablespoons Vegetable Juice Dressing (page 20) or Horseradish
    Mayonnaise (page 22)
salt and freshly ground pepper, to taste

1. Place the shrimp, cucumber, tomatoes, carrot, onion, and green pepper in a large bowl; toss to combine.

2. Pour the dressing onto the salad; season with salt and pepper; toss well. Pack the salad in plastic containers with tight-fitting lids.

Makes 2 servings

Chapter Six

FOR THE KIDS

Kids are a tough crowd to please when it comes to food. Their lunch bag must be filled with foods that look good, are fun to eat, and taste good. And, of course, a sweet treat is a must. If their meal does not reach these standards, kids simply do not eat it. We know it is a challenge to offer new and interesting foods, and keep tabs on high-fat, high-calorie, and high-sugar foods.

My suggestion is to stay calm and be flexible. The recipes and tips in this chapter will put you well on your way to feeding your little ones in a healthful, nutritious way and having them enjoy it too! Good luck.

TACO POCKETS

1/4 pound diced, cooked roast beef, chicken, or turkey

1/4 cup shredded low-fat cheddar cheese

1/2 cup canned black, kidney, or cannelloni beans, rinsed and drained

1/4 cup chopped red onion

1/2 cup shredded lettuce

1/4 cup prepared salsa

2 small pita breads

1. Combine the roast beef, cheese, beans, onion, and lettuce in a large bowl; toss gently.

2. Add the salsa; mix until well combined.

3. Gently open the pita breads; stuff the salad inside. Wrap tightly in aluminum foil.

Pack Along

- Baked Tortilla Chips (page 110)
- fruit juice box

Makes 2 sandwiches

PEANUT BUTTER, POTATO CHIP, AND SMOKED HAM SANDWICH

2 tablespoons chunky peanut butter

4 slices thick white bread

1/4 cup potato chips, broken into pieces

2 slices smoked ham, bacon strips, or turkey, thinly sliced

1. Spread the peanut butter on two slices of the bread.

2. Sprinkle the chips over the peanut butter. Top with the ham.

3. Gently close the sandwiches; cut in half crosswise. Wrap tightly in aluminum foil.

Makes 2 sandwiches

CHOCOLATE CHIP-CREAM CHEESE SANDWICH

A small amount of chocolate chips turn an ordinary sandwich into a treat.

1/4 cup plain cream cheese, softened
2 tablespoons chocolate chips
4 slices Banana Bread (page 9) or
    2 mini-bagels, split in half
1/2 sliced banana (optional)

1. Combine the cream cheese and chocolate chips in a small bowl; mix to blend.

2. Spread the cream cheese mixture on two slices of Banana Bread. Top with the banana slices. Gently close the sandwiches; cut in half crosswise. Wrap tightly in aluminum foil.

Makes 2 sandwiches

Pack Along

Flavored Popcorn
(page 111) or pretzels

Tip

Cut out sandwiches with cookie cutters. They are really fun to eat and take only a few extra seconds to prepare. Perfect for the kid who won't eat crust.

Tip

The critical element to the perfect kid lunch is the lunch box. Here are some tips:

- Let your kids pick it out.
- Purchase an insulated bag and thermos.
- Wash it on a daily basis.

MOCK FRANKFURTERS

Finally, a healthy frank.

1/4 cup peanut butter
2 tablespoons raisins
2 hot dog rolls
2 tablespoons granola, finely chopped
2 tablespoons shredded coconut or chopped nuts (optional)
2 bananas

1. Combine the peanut butter and raisins in a small bowl; mix well.

2. Spread the peanut butter mixture on the insides of the hot dog rolls. Sprinkle on granola and coconut. Wrap in aluminum foil.

3. At serving time, place the bananas in the rolls and press lightly.

Makes 2 sandwiches

Pack Along

- fresh fruit
- small container of yogurt for heartier appetites
- Flavored Popcorn (page 111)
- Hold the chips!

Surprise!!—Kids love to find something extra special in their lunch boxes. Here are some ideas:

- Pack a sheet of stickers.
- Tie ribbons around the plastic containers.
- Pack a note that says "You're the greatest" or "I love you."
- Send heart-shaped cookies.
- Send a photograph of someone special.
- Add some chocolate chips to a bag of raisins.

CHICKEN SALAD BURRITOS

This is a great way to use up small amounts of leftover vegetables, beans, rice, or meat.

$^1/_2$ cup cubed cooked chicken

$^1/_4$ cup canned black beans, rinsed and drained

$^1/_4$ cup canned corn kernels, drained

$^1/_4$ cup shredded cheese, any flavor

$^1/_4$ cup shredded carrot

$^1/_4$ cup creamy salad dressing, any variety

2 tablespoons sweet pickle relish

$^1/_4$ cup shredded lettuce

4 flour tortillas

Tip

To prevent a soggy tortilla, pack the filling and tortilla separately and have the kids assemble it at lunchtime. It's very easy. Don't forget a plastic fork or spoon.

1. Combine the chicken, beans, corn, cheese, and carrot in a mixing bowl; mix well. Add the dressing and pickle relish; toss to combine.

2. Spoon one-fourth of the chicken mixture at the end of each tortilla. Top with one-fourth of the lettuce and roll up to close. Secure with a toothpick. Wrap tightly in aluminum foil.

Makes 2 servings

SALAD CONES

Say yes to a cone for lunch—if it's filled with a nutritious salad. Don't forget to pack a spoon for scooping the salad into the ice cream cone.

1 cup Tuna Salad (page 7), Chicken Salad (page 8), Egg Salad (page 8), or your favorite sandwich filling

2 wafer ice cream cones with flat bottoms

Pack Along

- vegetable sticks
- Chocolate Chip–Pecan Cookies (page 103)

1. Pack ingredients separately in plastic containers with tight-fitting lids.

2. Before serving, scoop half of the salad into one ice cream cone.

Makes 2 servings

CHICKEN NUGGET PITAS

This lunch will be a favorite for the kid that loves fast-food chicken nuggets.

1/4 cup shredded lettuce

1/4 cup shredded carrots

2 pita breads, tops trimmed

6 chicken nuggets, cooked according to package directions

1/4 cup choice of dressing: Tahini Dressing (page 18), Honey Mustard (page 24), ranch, buttermilk, or any Flavored Mayonnaise (pages 21–23)

Pack Along

Spicy Apple Squares (page 107)

1. In a small bowl, combine lettuce and carrots.

2. Stuff each pita pocket with half of the chicken and half of the carrot-and-lettuce mixture. Wrap the pita tightly in aluminum foil. Pack the dressing separately. Before serving, top the pita with the dressing.

Makes 2 sandwiches

MEAT AND CHEESE ROLL-UPS

These are fun to make and eat. Since they can easily be unrolled, roll-ups are perfect for kids that like to eat each ingredient separately.

I tablespoon mustard or mayonnaise

4 slices any variety luncheon meat

4 soft breadsticks

4 slices any variety cheese

4 large lettuce leaves

Pack Along

Chocolate Chip–Pecan Cookies (page 103)

Spread a thin layer of mustard on one side of each piece of luncheon meat. Wrap a piece of luncheon meat around each bread stick, following with cheese and lettuce. Secure layers with a toothpick. Wrap tightly in aluminum foil.

Makes 2 sandwiches

CHEDDAR CHEESE AND SMOKED TURKEY MUFFINWICH

Instead of corn bread, wow the kids with a corn muffin sandwich. Experiment with different types of muffins to create your own "muffinwich."

unsalted butter or Flavored Mustard (page 24)
2 corn muffins, split in half
2 slices smoked turkey
2 slices cheddar cheese

1. Lightly butter one side of each corn muffin half.

2. Layer the turkey and cheese on the bottom halves. Gently close the sandwiches.

Makes 2 sandwiches

Pack Along
fresh fruit

Variations

Other muffin fillings:
- Flavored Cream Cheese (pages 14–15) mixed with nuts or granola
- cheese and apple slices
- bacon bits and cheese
- Poached Chicken Breasts (page 2) and Honey Mustard (page 24)
- ham and cheddar cheese

POACHED CHICKEN CROISSANDWICH

2 tablespoons mayonnaise or Flavored Mayonnaise (pages 21–23)
2 croissants, split in half
2 Poached Chicken Breasts (page 2), whole
2 slices Swiss, Muenster, Cheddar, or American cheese
2 large lettuce leaves
2 slices tomato

1. Spread the mayonnaise on the insides of the croissants.

2. Layer the bottom halves with chicken, cheese, lettuce, and tomato.

3. Gently close the sandwiches. Wrap tightly in aluminum foil.

Makes 2 sandwiches

Variations

Other kid-friendly croissant fillings:
- Waldorf Salad (page 48)
- roast beef and cheese
- Chunky Fruit Cream Cheese (page 14)
- Egg Salad (page 8)
- Tuna Salad (page 7)
- assorted cold cuts

Tip

Smile! Kids who need a little coaxing at mealtime will love a croissant decorated with raisin or cucumber eyes, parsley or alfalfa sprout hair, and a cheese-stick nose. Attach with toothpicks. Pack a few smiling face stickers, a note that says "smile," and a chocolate kiss to complete the theme.

Chapter Seven

LEFTOVERS

Whether part of Tuesday's dinner or the weekend barbecue, small quantities of leftover food—which often end up in the garbage—can happily satisfy you at lunchtime instead. The trick is recycling the leftovers by adding ingredients, thus creating different tasting dishes.

The recipes in this chapter are inexpensive and so delicious you will forget the main ingredient is something you recently ate for dinner. Your leftovers will be good to the last bite!

LUSCIOUS LEFTOVER INGREDIENTS

The following is a list of leftovers that are really good in salads and sandwiches. Store in clear, tightly covered plastic containers so you won't forget about them.

rice, any variety

beans, any variety

vegetables, canned, fresh, or frozen (packed separately, if possible)

pasta, any variety

cooked meat, pork, turkey, fish, or chicken; any amount

cooked potatoes

meat loaf

meatballs

fajitas

chili

coleslaw, potato salad

spaghetti and tomato sauce or meat sauce

stir-fried vegetables

leftover Chinese take-out food

TURKEY AND CRANBERRY SAUCE ON PUMPKIN BREAD

1 to 2 tablespoons canned whole berry
    cranberry sauce or cranberry relish
1/4 cup mayonnaise
4 slices Pumpkin Bread (page 10)
2 to 4 thick slices leftover cooked boneless
    turkey breast, skinned
4 Boston lettuce leaves

Tip

You can substitute cooked turkey for chicken in most recipes.

1. Combine the cranberry sauce and mayonnaise in a small bowl; mix together. Spread the cranberry mixture on two slices of the Pumpkin Bread.

2. Layer the bread evenly with the turkey and lettuce.

3. Gently close the sandwiches; cut in half crosswise. Wrap tightly in aluminum foil.

Makes 2 servings

Pack Along
- vegetable sticks
- fresh fruit

Variations

Other terrific turkey combinations to try:
- turkey and Swiss cheese
- turkey, bacon, and Swiss cheese
- turkey and blue cheese
- turkey, brie, sun-dried tomatoes, and Honey Mustard (page 24)
- turkey, apple slices, and cheddar cheese
- smoked turkey and Jarlsberg cheese
- turkey, havarti cheese, and Russian dressing
- smoked turkey, smoked gouda cheese, and Herb Mayonnaise (page 23)

TURKEY SLAW ROLLS

4 ounces cooked turkey, cut into thin slices
1/2 cup coleslaw
2 tablespoons mayonnaise
2 rolls or baguettes, split
4 thin tomato slices
1 cup shredded lettuce

Serving Suggestion

To avoid sogginess with a moist filling such as this, pack bread and filling separately and assemble the sandwich at serving time.

1. Combine the turkey, coleslaw, and mayonnaise in a small bowl. Pack in containers with tight-fitting lids. Pack tomato slices, shredded lettuce, and rolls separately.

2. Upon serving, evenly divide turkey mixture on the bottoms of the rolls. Top with tomato slices and shredded lettuce.

3. Gently close the sandwiches; cut in half crosswise.

Makes 2 sandwiches

Tip

Save that little bit of leftover coleslaw from the weekend barbecue. It makes a great sandwich topping without a lot of fuss.

Variation

Try this version: roast beef or leftover steak strips, Swiss cheese, and coleslaw on a baguette.

TACO SALAD

1/2 pound leftover chicken, turkey, steak strips, or roast beef, cut into thin slices

1 jar (12 ounces) prepared salsa

2 1/2 cups small pieces romaine lettuce

1 cup tortilla chips or Baked Tortilla Chips (page 110)

1/2 cup cherry tomatoes, halved

1/3 cup shredded cheddar cheese

Tips

- Any combination of leftover chicken or beef will work well in this salad.
- To ensure crunchy chips, add them just before serving if the salad will be sitting more than a few hours.

1. Combine the chicken with the salsa in a large bowl; mix well. Set aside.

2. Combine the lettuce, chips, tomatoes, and cheese in a large bowl; toss gently.

3. Pack the lettuce mixture and the salsa mixture separately in plastic containers with tight-fitting lids.

4. Before serving, top the lettuce mixture with the salsa mixture.

Makes 2 servings

BARBECUED CHICKEN AND GOAT CHEESE SALAD

1 cup leftover shredded barbecued chicken

2 cups torn Boston lettuce, or any variety

1 red bell pepper, cut into 1/2" strips

3 ounces soft goat cheese, crumbled

Lemon-Mustard Dressing (page 17)

1/2 cup walnuts

Tip

Use the leftover chicken from the weekend barbecue or make extra for this delicious salad.

1. Combine the chicken, lettuce, bell pepper, and goat cheese in a large bowl; toss lightly.

2. Pack the chicken mixture in plastic containers with tight-fitting lids. Pack the dressing and walnuts separately.

3. Before serving, dress the salad and gently toss; garnish with nuts.

Makes 2 servings

ROAST BEEF AND POTATO SALAD

¹/₂ pound cooked small red potatoes or leftover baked or boiled
    potatoes, quartered

4 ounces leftover roast beef, thinly sliced

¹/₄ cup chopped red onion

2 small plum tomatoes, seeded and chopped

¹/₄ cup Balsamic or Red Wine Vinaigrette
    (page 17), Sweet Asian Dressing
    (page 18), or mayonnaise

salt and freshly ground black pepper, to
    taste

2 cups torn romaine lettuce

Pack Along

- crusty bread or flat breads
- Chocolate Chip–Toffee Bar Brownie (page 96)

1. Combine the potatoes, roast beef, onion, and tomatoes in a large bowl; mix well. Add the dressing; toss to coat. Season with salt and pepper.

2. Pack the lettuce in plastic containers with tight-fitting lids. Top the lettuce with the potato mixture.

Makes 2 servings

Moneysaving Tip

A few slices of leftover cooked meats go a long way in a salad or sandwich; save them for a meal instead of making them food for Fido.

Variation

For a hot sandwich, just pack leftover roast beef or turkey slices in a microwavable container, top with gravy or beef bouillon, and microwave at High until hot. Serve over rye or white bread.

GYRO

This delicious version of a classic Greek favorite will delight the brown bagger who enjoys street-vendor food.

2 pita breads
4 ounces leftover roast beef or beef
     tenderloin, cut into thin strips
1/4 cup thinly sliced cucumber
1/4 cup thinly sliced red onion
1/2 cup shredded iceberg lettuce
2 slices tomato, chopped
1 tablespoon chopped fresh
     parsley
Dill-Yogurt Dressing (page 21)

1. Open the pita rounds. Fill each pocket with equal amounts of the roast beef, cucumber, red onion, lettuce, and tomato. Garnish with parsley.

2. Wrap each sandwich tightly in aluminum foil. Pack the dressing in small plastic containers with tight-fitting lids. Before serving, pour the dressing on the sandwich.

Makes 2 sandwiches

Pack Along

- **Dried Fruit Compote (page 102)**
- **Strawberry-Chocolate Shortbread Bars (page 101)**

Tip

After slicing off the tops of your pita bread, instead of throwing them away, stuff them into the bottom of the pita pocket. The extra bit of bread will absorb any extra dressing from the sandwich, helping the whole pocket to stay intact and not "bottom out."

MEAT LOAF AND PASTA SALAD

1 cup leftover cooked pasta
1/2 cup chopped and seeded tomato
1/3 cup Balsamic or Red Wine Vinaigrette
   (page 17)
1 tablespoon Dijon mustard
1 cup cold cooked meat loaf, cubed
2 tablespoons grated Parmesan cheese

Pack Along

**Mocha Chip Brownies
(page 98)**

1. Mix together the pasta and tomato in a large bowl.

2. Combine the vinaigrette with the mustard in a small bowl; whisk together. Pour the dressing mixture over the pasta; toss to coat.

3. Add the meat loaf; toss gently. Sprinkle with the cheese.

4. Pack in plastic containers with tight-fitting lids.

Makes 2 servings

Tip

Moneysaving

Toss plain leftover cooked pasta with 1 teaspoon of oil. Refrigerate in an airtight container for up to a week.

Variations

For cold meat loaf lunches:

- Layer on a hero roll with lots of ketchup. Add crushed potato chips—kids will love it.
- Chop and mix with salsa.
- Chop and mix with componata.

SOUTHWESTERN RICE SALAD

1/2 cup cooked rice (any variety)
1 cup leftover cooked turkey, roast beef, or chicken, cubed
1/2 cup corn kernels
1/2 cup red bell pepper or Roasted Peppers (page 4), finely chopped
2 tablespoons chopped red onion
1 small jalapeño pepper, finely chopped
Southwestern Dressing (page 20)
1 tablespoon chopped fresh cilantro
salt and freshly ground black pepper, to taste
2 cups red leaf lettuce

Variation

1. Combine the rice, turkey, corn, bell pepper, onion, and jalapeño pepper in a large bowl; toss gently.

Add black beans or substitute them for the rice.

2. Add the Southwestern Dressing to the rice mixture; toss gently to coat. Top with the cilantro. Season with salt and pepper. Pack the lettuce in plastic containers with tight-fitting lids; top with the rice salad.

Makes 2 servings

Timesaving Tip

Leftover Mexican rice with beans gives this salad extra flavor without a lot of fuss.

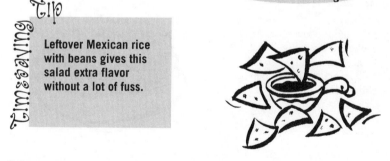

Tip

Removing corn kernels from the cob: Firmly hold the cob vertically over a plate. Using a serrated knife, cut downward to remove the corn from the cob. The kernels will fall in a pile on the plate. You can eat them raw, steamed, or sautéed.

MINCED ROAST BEEF SANDWICH

1/2 cup minced roast beef
2 tablespoons finely chopped cucumber
2 tablespoons Chutney Dressing (page 17)
1/4 cup cream cheese
4 thick slices black bread, rye, or whole
   wheat bread

Tip

Minced leftover meat or poultry is an easy way to hide tough meat or stretch a small amount of leftovers. Add more vegetables if you need more volume.

1. Mix the roast beef, cucumber, and Chutney Dressing in a small bowl; mix to coat.

2. Spread the cream cheese on each slice of bread.

3. Spread the roast beef mixture evenly on two of the bread slices. Gently close the sandwiches; cut in half crosswise. Wrap tightly in aluminum foil.

Makes 2 sandwiches

Serving Suggestions

Try Minced Roast Beef with:

- Horseradish Mayonnaise (page 22)
- minced celery and Dijon mustard
- nuts
- chopped fruit
- chopped vegetables

Moneysaving Tip

Even the smallest amount of meat, poultry, or fish can be combined with carrots, celery, red onion, pickle relish, and so on, seasoned with flavored mustard or mayonnaise, and spread on good-quality bread to create a delicious sandwich for very little money.

ASIAN ROAST BEEF SALAD

Any leftover meat, poultry, or vegetable will work in this salad.

1/4 cup snow peas, ends trimmed, blanched (page 46)
1/4 cup broccoli florets, blanched (page 46)
1/4 cup thinly sliced carrots
1/4 cup sliced scallions
1/2 cup shredded lettuce
1 cup leftover roast beef, cut into thin strips
Sweet Asian Dressing (page 18)
1/4 cup thin crisp Chinese noodles

Variation

1. Combine the snow peas, broccoli, carrots, scallions, lettuce, and roast beef in a large bowl; toss to combine.

Feel free to throw in some leftover pasta or cooked rice.

2. Pack the salad into plastic containers with tight-fitting lids. Pack the dressing and noodles separately. Before serving, pour the dressing on the salad and gently toss; garnish with the noodles.

Makes 2 servings

Pack Along

• Strawberry-Chocolate Shortbread Bars (page 101)
• canned mandarin orange sections

Tip

Freeze leftovers in individual portions. Have them for lunch in a few weeks. They'll taste as good as new.

Chapter Eight

COOKIES, BROWNIES, AND TREATS

For most of us, half the fun of eating lunch is getting to the dessert—not being able to wait to reach into the brown bag, open the wrapper, and sink your teeth into a sweet treat to finish off the meal. No matter what the age or eating habits, packing a homemade treat shows your someone special you care, even if that person is yourself.

The recipes in this chapter taste wonderful, yet are so simple to follow you'll want to make them all the time. And why not? Some are even low in fat, so indulge. Pack a little love into each lunch. After all, what's better than finding a special treat at the bottom of your brown bag?

CHOCOLATE CHIP-TOFFEE BAR BROWNIES

2 cups all-purpose flour
1 teaspoon baking powder
$^1/_2$ teaspoon salt
1$^3/_4$ cups firmly packed brown sugar
$^3/_4$ cup unsalted butter, at room temperature
2 eggs
2 tablespoons coffee liqueur or 1 teaspoon vanilla
$^1/_2$ cup semisweet chocolate chips
$^3/_4$ cup chopped chocolate-covered English toffee bars

1. Preheat the oven to 350°F. Grease an 8-inch square baking pan.

2. Combine the flour, baking powder, and salt in a small bowl. Set aside.

3. Cream the brown sugar and butter in a large bowl. Add the eggs and coffee liqueur; beat until light and smooth.

4. Add the flour mixture; beat until just combined at low speed.

5. Stir in the chocolate chips and $^1/_2$ cup of the chopped toffee bars. Spread evenly into the prepared pan.

6. Bake until a wooden tester inserted in the center comes out clean, 35 minutes. Sprinkle immediately with the remaining chopped toffee bars. Cool completely on wire rack. Cut into 9 bars.

Tips

Makes 9 brownies

- Cool brownies and bar cookies completely in their pan before cutting into squares.
- Cut brownies or bar cookies with a serrated knife. First, cut around perimeter of the pan and then cut into bars. Remove with a spatula as needed. They will stay fresh for up to 5 days.
- To freeze, wrap brownies or bar cookies in tightly covered plastic containers or airtight freezer bags. Aluminum foil or plastic wrap will also work, but make sure the packages are tightly sealed to prevent freezer burn or smell.
- Be creative: Vary the chips and nuts in cookie and brownie recipes to make personal favorites.

WHITE CHOCOLATE CHIP COOKIES

$^1/_2$ cup unsalted butter, at room temperature

$^1/_3$ cup granulated sugar

$^1/_3$ cup firmly packed brown sugar

1 egg

1 teaspoon vanilla extract

1 cup all-purpose flour

$^1/_4$ teaspoon baking soda

$^1/_2$ teaspoon baking powder

$^1/_4$ teaspoon salt

$^3/_4$ cup white chocolate chips

$^3/_4$ cup macadamia nuts or pecans, coarsely chopped (optional)

1. Preheat the oven to 375°F. Grease the cookie sheets.

2. Cream the butter and sugars in a large bowl. Add the egg and vanilla; mix until light and fluffy.

3. Add the flour, baking soda, baking powder, and salt to the butter mixture; mix until just combined.

4. Stir in the chocolate and nuts. Mix well.

5. For large cookies, drop dough by $^1/_3$ cupfuls about two inches apart onto cookie sheets. For smaller cookies, drop the dough by tablespoons onto cookie sheets.

6. Bake until the cookies begin to brown around the edges, about 15 minutes. Cool 4 minutes; remove from cookie sheet; transfer to wire racks to cool completely. Store in airtight containers or freeze up to 3 weeks.

Tips

- Freeze brownies or cookies in individual serving packages. Simply drop into your brown bag as needed. By lunchtime they will have thawed.

- To prevent cookies from breaking, wrap in aluminum foil and place in a self-sealing plastic bag or plastic container with a tight-fitting lid. Then pack.

Makes 9 large or 20 small cookies

MOCHA CHIP BROWNIES

1/2 cup unsalted butter

2 ounces unsweetened chocolate, chopped

1 teaspoon instant coffee powder

1 cup sugar

2/3 cup all-purpose flour

1/2 teaspoon baking powder

2 large eggs

1 teaspoon vanilla

1/2 cup white chocolate chips

1. Preheat the oven to 350°F. Grease an 8-inch square baking pan.

2. Combine the butter and chocolate in a small saucepan; cook over low heat until melted. Stir in the coffee until dissolved. Set aside to cool.

3. Mix the sugar, flour, and baking powder in a medium-size mixing bowl.

4. Add the chocolate mixture, eggs, and vanilla to the sugar mixture; mix well. Stir in the chips.

5. Spoon the batter into the prepared pan. Bake until a wooden tester inserted into the center comes out with a few moist crumbs attached, 25 minutes. Cool in the pan on a rack. Cut into 9 squares.

Variation

Omit the coffee powder for chocolate chip brownies.

Makes 9 brownies

Cooking Tip

Use the microwave to melt the butter and chocolate easily, place them in a microwavable dish; cook on High for 2 minutes. Stir; continue cooking on High until smooth, about 1 more minute.

S'MORE BROWNIES

This has all the ingredients of the childhood favorite wrapped up in a neat brownie.

2 cups coarsely ground graham cracker crumbs
1²/₃ cups sweetened condensed milk
1 cup mini semisweet chocolate chips
12 large marshmallows, cut crosswise in half
1 ounce milk chocolate or semisweet chocolate, grated

1. Preheat the oven to 350°F. Grease an 8-inch square baking pan.

2. Combine the graham cracker crumbs, sweetened condensed milk, and mini chocolate chips in a large bowl. Pour the batter into the prepared pan.

3. Bake until lightly browned, 25 minutes. Carefully place the marshmallows on top of the hot brownies, spacing evenly. Cover tightly with foil and let stand 15 minutes.

4. Remove the foil from the pan. Spread the melted marshmallows evenly on top of the brownies. Top with grated chocolate. Cool completely on a wire rack. Cut into squares.

Makes about 16 brownies

RASPBERRY-OATMEAL BARS

nonstick cooking spray

1 cup all-purpose flour

$3/4$ cup rolled oats

$1/2$ cup firmly packed brown sugar

$1/2$ cup unsalted butter, melted

$1/2$ cup granola cereal

$1/2$ teaspoon baking soda

$1/2$ teaspoon vanilla

$3/4$ cup semisweet chocolate chips

$2/3$ cup raspberry preserves

1. Preheat the oven to 350° F. Spray a 9-inch square baking pan with nonstick cooking spray.

2. Combine the flour, oats, sugar, butter, $1/4$ cup of the cereal, baking soda, vanilla, and chocolate chips in a large bowl; mix well.

3. Press one-half of the mixture evenly onto the bottom of the prepared pan. Set remaining mixture aside.

4. Drop the preserves by the tablespoonful gently into the pan to cover bottom.

5. Add the remaining cereal to the reserved oat mixture; mix together. Pour the oat mixture over the preserves; press lightly to flatten.

6. Bake until lightly browned, 30 minutes. Cool in a pan on a wire rack. Cut into bars.

Makes about 12 bars

Variations

Add $1/2$ cup raisins to the crumb mixture.

Substitutions for raspberry preserves:

- cooked apple chunks sprinkled with sugar and lemon
- 1 cup prune purée
- your favorite flavor jam or preserve

STRAWBERRY-CHOCOLATE SHORTBREAD BARS

Strawberries and chocolate—a classic combination combined in a delicious bar. This is perfect when you want something sweet.

1 cup unsalted butter, at room temperature
2 cups all-purpose flour
1/2 cup confectioners' sugar
1 teaspoon vanilla
3/4 cup strawberry preserves
1 tablespoon milk
1 tablespoon unsalted butter
1/4 cup semisweet chocolate chips

1. Preheat the oven to 350° F. Grease a 9-inch square baking pan.

2. Cream the 1 cup butter, flour, confectioners' sugar, and vanilla in a large bowl until a dough holds together. Divide the dough into two equal balls; flatten each ball into a circle large enough to fit into the pan. Wrap and refrigerate for 30 minutes.

3. Press one circle into the bottom of the prepared pan and about 3/4 inch up the sides. Roll the other disk to a 9-inch square, 1/4-inch thick.

4. Spread the strawberry preserves over the dough in the pan. Cover with the remaining dough. Pinch down side edges all around the pan.

5. Bake at 350° F. until golden brown and firm to the touch. Cool completely.

6. While the bars are cooling, combine the milk and 1 tablespoon butter in a small saucepan; cook over medium heat until the butter is completely melted. Remove from the heat and stir in the chocolate chips until melted. Drizzle the chocolate over the bars. Let set. Cut into squares.

Makes about 20 small bars

LEMON BARS

1 cup unsalted butter, at room temperature

2 cups all-purpose flour

1/2 cup confectioners' sugar

4 large eggs

1/4 cup all-purpose flour

2 cups granulated sugar

6 tablespoons freshly squeezed lemon juice

1/2 teaspoon salt

1 teaspoon baking powder

grated zest of 1 lemon*

1. Preheat the oven to 350° F. Grease a 9 × 13–inch baking pan. Combine the butter, 2 cups flour, and confectioners' sugar in a mixing bowl; cream until dough holds together. Press dough evenly into pan, making 1/4-inch edges and a 3/4-inch bottom. Bake for 20 minutes. Remove from oven.

2. Meanwhile, whisk together remaining ingredients. Pour the mixture over the dough. Spread evenly. Bake until set and light brown, 20 minutes. Cool completely before cutting. Refrigerate bars in an airtight container up to 5 days.

Makes 12 to 14 bars

DRIED FRUIT COMPOTE

1/2 cup mixed dried fruit (apricots, prunes, pears, apples, and/or figs)

1/4 cup water

1 tablespoon orange juice

1 lemon slice

1. Place all the ingredients in a saucepan. Bring to a boil, lower heat, and simmer until fruit is tender, about 20 minutes. Let cool. Pour into a plastic container, cover tightly, and refrigerate until cold.

2. Pack fruit compote into plastic containers with tight-fitting lids.

Makes 2 servings

* The zest of the lemon is the outermost peel without any of the pith (white membrane). To remove zest, use a zester or the fine side of a vegetable grater.

CHOCOLATE CHIP-PECAN COOKIES

$^1/_2$ cup unsalted butter, at room temperature

$^2/_3$ cup firmly packed brown sugar

I egg

I teaspoon vanilla

I cup all-purpose flour

$^1/_2$ teaspoon baking soda

$^1/_4$ teaspoon baking powder

$^1/_4$ teaspoon salt

I cup semisweet chocolate chips or chocolate chunks

I cup chopped pecans

Tip

Never store different cookies in the same jar. Within a day, they will start to take on each other's flavors.

1. Preheat the oven to 325°F.

2. In the bowl of a food processor, place the butter, brown sugar, egg, and vanilla. Process for about 2 minutes.

3. Add the flour, baking soda, baking powder, and salt. Pulse (short on/off bursts) until just combined. Transfer to a mixing bowl.

4. Add the chocolate chips and nuts; mix until just combined.

5. Drop dough by rounded tablespoonfuls onto ungreased cookie sheets about 2 inches apart. Bake 15 minutes. Cool completely on wire racks.

Variation

Substitute macadamia nuts for pecans.

Makes 18 cookies

Cooking Tip

If you don't have a food processor, cream the butter and sugar in a large bowl. Add the egg and vanilla. Mix well. Blend in the dry ingredients and follow the rest of the recipe.

ORANGE BISCOTTI WITH PINE NUTS

1/2 cup unsalted butter

3/4 cup sugar

2 eggs

2 tablespoons orange juice

2 tablespoons grated orange zest*

1 teaspoon vanilla

2 1/4 cups all-purpose flour

1 1/2 teaspoons baking powder

1/4 teaspoon salt

1 cup pine nuts, toasted

Tip

Toasting nuts: Place nuts in a shallow baking pan and bake at 350° F. for 8 minutes or until fragrant.

1. Preheat the oven to 350° F. Grease and flour a large baking sheet.

2. Cream the butter and sugar together in a large bowl until light and fluffy.

3. Add the eggs, orange juice, orange zest, and vanilla; beat well.

4. Combine the flour, baking powder, and salt in a small bowl. Add the flour mixture to the butter mixture; blend thoroughly. Add the nuts; mix well.

5. Divide the dough in half. Shape each half into a log 12 inches long, 1/2 inch high, and 2 inches wide. Place on prepared baking sheet.

6. Bake until lightly browned, 25 minutes. Let cool for 5 minutes and transfer to a clean work surface.

7. Cut loaf diagonally, with a serrated knife, into slices 1/2 inch thick. Lay the slices flat on a baking sheet and bake for 5 minutes; remove from the oven. Turn the slices over; return to the oven and bake until light brown, 5 minutes. Store biscotti in airtight containers for up to 2 weeks.

Makes about 4 dozen biscotti

* The zest of the orange is the outermost peel without any of the pith (white membrane). To remove zest, use a zester or the fine side of a vegetable grater.

PEANUT BUTTER-CHOCOLATE CHIP COOKIES

Forget the Reeses. This is the ultimate peanut butter–chocolate treat.

1/2 cup unsalted butter, at room temperature
3/4 cup chunky peanut butter
I cup firmly packed light brown sugar
2 eggs
1 1/2 teaspoons vanilla
1 1/2 cups flour
I teaspoon baking powder
1/2 cup roasted peanuts, chopped
I cup semisweet chocolate chips

1. Preheat the oven to 350°F. Grease the baking sheets.

2. Cream the butter, peanut butter, and brown sugar until light.

3. Add the eggs, one at a time, beating well after each addition. Add the vanilla; beat well.

4. Stir the flour and baking powder together in a small bowl. Add the flour mixture, 1/4 cup at a time, to the peanut butter mixture; stir well after each addition.

5. Mix in the chopped peanuts and chocolate chips.

6. Drop dough by rounded tablespoonfuls about 2 inches apart onto cookie sheets. Bake until light brown, 8 to 10 minutes. Cool completely on wire racks.

Makes 2 dozen cookies

LOW-FAT CARROT SQUARES

These squares will delight carrot cake lovers with a lot less fat and cholesterol than traditional recipes.

nonstick cooking spray
1 cup whole wheat flour
1 cup all-purpose flour
1 3/4 cups sugar
2 teaspoons baking soda
2 teaspoons cinnamon
1 teaspoon baking powder
1/2 teaspoon salt
1 can (8 ounces) crushed pineapple, drained
3/4 cup nonfat plain yogurt
1 egg
1/2 tablespoon vanilla
1/4 cup vegetable oil
1 cup cooked carrots, puréed
1/4 cup raisins
1/2 cup chopped walnuts

Serving Suggestion

For Easy Cream Cheese Frosting: Combine 1/2 cup light cream cheese, 1/4 cup butter, 1 teaspoon vanilla, and 1 1/2 cups confectioners' sugar. Spread over cooled squares.

1. Preheat the oven to 350° F. Spray a 9×13–inch baking pan with nonstick cooking spray.

2. Combine the whole wheat flour, all-purpose flour, sugar, baking soda, cinnamon, baking powder, and salt in a large bowl; mix well.

3. Add the pineapple, yogurt, egg, vanilla, and oil; mix well to combine.

4. Stir in the carrots, raisins, and nuts.

5. Pour batter into the prepared pan. Bake until golden brown and springy to the touch, 40 minutes. Cool completely and cut into squares.

Makes 30 bars

SPICY APPLE SQUARES

1/2 cup unsalted butter, at room temperature
1/2 cup granulated sugar
1/2 cup firmly packed brown sugar
1 egg
1 cup all-purpose flour
1/2 teaspoon baking powder
1/4 teaspoon salt
1/2 teaspoon cinnamon
pinch nutmeg
pinch mace
2 apples, peeled, cored, and chopped
1/2 cup chopped walnuts or raisins

1. Preheat the oven to 350° F. Grease an 8-inch square baking pan.

2. Cream the butter and sugars together. Add the egg; mix well.

3. Combine the flour, baking powder, salt, cinnamon, nutmeg, and mace together in a small bowl. Add the flour mixture to the butter mixture; mix well.

4. Gently stir in the apples and nuts. Spread batter evenly into the pan.

5. Bake until a wooden tester comes out of the center clean, 35 minutes.

Makes 12 squares

OATMEAL-RAISIN COOKIES

1 cup unsalted butter, at room temperature
1 cup dark brown sugar
3/4 cup granulated sugar
2 eggs
1 teaspoon vanilla
1 cup all-purpose flour
1 cup whole wheat flour
1 teaspoon baking soda
1/2 teaspoon salt
1 teaspoon cinnamon
2 cups old-fashioned or quick-cooking rolled
   oats
1 1/2 cups raisins
3/4 cup walnuts, chopped

Variation

Add 3/4 cup chocolate chips for extra sweetness.

1. Preheat the oven to 350° F. Grease the cookie sheets.

2. Cream together the butter and sugars. Add the eggs and vanilla; beat well.

3. Combine the flours, baking soda, salt, and cinnamon together in a small bowl. Add the flour mixture to the butter mixture; mix well.

4. Add the remaining ingredients; blend well.

5. Drop dough by 1/3 cupfuls about 2 inches apart onto cookie sheets. Bake 12 to 15 minutes.

Makes about 15 cookies

LOW-FAT WALNUT-CHOCOLATE CHIP BISCOTTI

These crisp cookies are perfect dipped in coffee or tea. And they have the added plus of having no butter.

1 egg
1/2 cup sugar
1 1/2 teaspoons vanilla
3/4 cup plus 2 tablespoons all-purpose flour
3/4 teaspoon baking powder
1 1/2 teaspoons instant espresso powder or instant coffee powder
3/4 teaspoon cinnamon
1/4 teaspoon salt
1/3 cup chocolate chips
1/3 cup chopped walnuts

1. Preheat the oven to 375° F. Grease a baking sheet.

2. Combine the egg and sugar in a mixing bowl; beat until light and thick. Add the vanilla; beat well.

3. Sift the dry ingredients together in a separate bowl; add the dry mixture to the egg mixture; beat well. Mix in the chocolate chips and walnuts.

4. Divide dough in half. Shape each half into a log 12 inches long, 1/2 inch high, and 2 inches wide. Place on prepared baking sheet. Bake until lightly browned, 20 minutes. Remove from oven; cool 5 minutes; transfer to a clean work surface.

5. Cut loaf diagonally, with a serrated knife, into slices 1/2 inch thick. Lay the slices flat on ungreased baking sheets and bake for 10 minutes. Turn over and bake for an additional 10 minutes. Cool completely. Store biscotti in airtight containers for up to 2 weeks.

Makes about 18 cookies

BAKED TORTILLA CHIPS

3 corn or flour tortillas, cut into eighths
butter-flavored cooking spray
1/2 teaspoon garlic powder
1/2 teaspoon ground cumin
salt and freshly ground black pepper, to taste

1. Preheat the oven to 350° F.

2. Place the tortilla wedges on a baking sheet.

3. Spray wedges with butter-flavored cooking spray.

4. Sprinkle on remaining ingredients.

5. Bake until crispy, about 12 minutes.

Makes 2 servings

Serving Suggestion

Perfect to eat with a small container of your favorite salsa or fat-free bean dip.

Tip

Double or triple the recipe and store in self-sealing plastic bags or plastic containers with tight-fitting lids for up to 1 month.

Variations

Omit seasonings and sprinkle on:
- 1 teaspoon of sugar and 1/2 teaspoon cinnamon
- 2 tablespoons grated Parmesan cheese, 1 teaspoon dried basil, and 1/2 teaspoon garlic powder, salt, and freshly ground black pepper to taste

FLAVORED POPCORN

Take some air-popped popcorn, add a little of this and a dash of that, toss to coat, and you have a gourmet snack that is low in fat and calories.

Cheesy Popcorn

2 cups warm air-popped popcorn
2 tablespoons reduced-calorie margarine, melted
3 tablespoons grated Parmesan or cheddar cheese
salt, pepper, and garlic powder, to taste

Combine all ingredients in a large bowl. Toss to coat evenly.

Calorie-Cutting Tip

Omit the margarine and spray popcorn with a nice coat of butter-flavored cooking spray

Dried Apple and Cinnamon Popcorn

2 cups warm air-popped popcorn
2 tablespoons reduced-calorie margarine, melted
1 cup dried apples, chopped
1 1/2 tablespoons sugar
1 teaspoon cinnamon

Combine all ingredients in a large bowl. Toss to coat evenly.

Pretzels and Popcorn

2 cups warm air-popped popcorn
1 cup unsalted pretzel nuggets or mini twists
2 tablespoons reduced-calorie margarine, melted
1 teaspoon dry Italian seasoning
2 tablespoons grated Parmesan cheese

Combine all ingredients in a large bowl. Toss to coat evenly.

Popcorn Candy Mix

2 cups air-popped popcorn
1 tablespoon sugar or vanilla sugar
1 cup jelly beans

Combine all ingredients in a large bowl. Toss to coat evenly.

INDEX